LISTENING DICTATIO

LISTENING DICTATION

Understanding English Sentence Structure

Joan Morley

*Under the Auspices of the English Language Institute
at the University of Michigan*

Ann Arbor   **The University of Michigan Press**

Copyright © by the University of Michigan 1976
All rights reserved
ISBN 0-472-08667-7
Library of Congress Catalog Card No. 75-31050
Published in the United States of America by
The University of Michigan Press
Manufactured in the United States of America

2000   1999   1998   1997   24   23   22   21

Acknowledgments

Many colleagues and students have contributed helpful ideas during the preparation of these materials. Particular appreciation goes to Albert Davis and David Firestone for language laboratory management of the materials and to James Bixler, studio engineer, for his work on the recording of the lessons. Special thanks go to Eleanor Foster for office management of the materials, and to Betsy Johnsmiller and Marla Bluestone for their work on the final draft of the manuscript.

Contents

WORKBOOK

ANSWER KEY

To the Teacher

This is the workbook for a series of thirty-two language laboratory lessons in *listening/writing/grammar*. Although the lessons originally were prepared exclusively for use in the laboratory, they can be read "live" by the teacher if language laboratory facilities are not available. The answer key can be used as the teacher's script (see pages 79–80).

The lessons were developed to reinforce basic English grammatical patterns after classroom presentation and practice. Although the lessons were written to correspond to the lesson sequence in *English Sentence Structure*, by Robert Krohn (published by The University of Michigan Press), they may be used as an independent set of supplementary/reinforcement materials or in conjunction with other grammar texts.

The purpose of these lessons is to develop basic skill in discriminative listening. Through carefully structured practice, the students improve their ability to extract meaning from spoken English sentences. They learn to attend to grammatical relationships within the flow of natural spoken English, with its patterns of contraction, word reduction, elision, assimilation, blending, phrasing, stress, rhythm, and intonation.

To accomplish the purpose, the two parts of each lesson have been sequenced in the following way. In part 1 the students—

> listen to the sentence,
> repeat it aloud,
> listen to the sentence again (and try to remember it),
> write the sentence,
> listen to the sentence a third time,
> check the sentence as they listen.

Part 1 focuses on listening to the "parts" of the sentence.

Part 2 focuses on listening to the "whole" sentence and extracting the grammatical relationships in order to understand the message. In part 2 the students—

> listen to the sentence (and try to remember it),
> rapidly read the three possible answers,
> circle the one answer they believe to be correct.

(The sentences in part 2 are the same sentences as in part 1, but have been randomly reordered.)

Each lesson requires active participation on the part of the students. They cannot be passively "detached." The lessons guide the students toward self-disciplined listening. Concentration and urgency for remembering are demanded by the structure of the lessons. The lessons stress memory—lengthening memory span and strengthening immediate recall. Students should be encouraged to repeat to themselves, and, in a sense, to try to "rehear." Immediate feedback about performance is provided through the answer key at the back of this book.

It is very important that students *check their answers* against the answer key immediately after completing a lesson. They should circle their mistakes, analyze their errors, and discuss them with their teacher. Particular attention should be given to—

> suffix errors or omissions (-ed, -es, -s, -'s, -ing, -ly, -er, -est),
> function word errors or omissions (articles, prepositions, conjunctions, pronouns, auxiliaries),
> spelling, punctuation, capitalization errors.

The series of thirty-two lessons is designed so that the level of difficulty increases gradually—

> in sentence length,
> in sentence complexity,
> in speed of delivery,
> in time allowed for writing.

SUGGESTIONS

When students have completed a lesson in the language laboratory and the types of errors they have made have been given classroom attention, it is useful production reinforcement to have oral practice of the sentences. Special attention can be given to natural spoken English with its patterns of—

> contractions, reductions, and assimilation,
> blending and phrasing,
> rhythm, stress, and intonation.

Some teachers write the sentences on the blackboard (or use an overhead projector) and use graphics (lines and symbols) to help students visualize these important aspects of spoken English as they practice.

Some students, particularly low-level students, will want to copy the sentences from the answer key into the workbook. They feel they are so poor in listening that they should copy the sentence before they hear it in order to "catch" it when they listen to it. This should be discouraged. This is not the intent of the book. Indeed, the intent is exactly the opposite—to have students listen carefully, to "catch" as much as they can, and *then* to check the answers to see what they did not hear.

USING THE FIRST LESSON

In order to introduce students to the format of the book many teachers like to read the first lesson "live" in class. As a follow-up, in order to demonstrate to students the importance of *checking* their answers and *circling in red* the listening gaps they have experienced, many teachers have students exchange books to check a classmate's answers. This is followed by a group grammatical error analysis charted on the blackboard by the teacher as students report the things they have *not* heard. This error analysis critique and discussion should be repeated after the class has completed each unit of four lessons and the teacher has checked and returned the students' workbooks.

In reading the first lesson the format found on pages 79 and 80 should be followed *exactly. Do not* repeat any more times than is indicated. Use a clear natural voice. Do not read word by word or exaggerate in any way. Phrasing and blending should be natural.

Instruct the students to listen carefully and "get" as much as they can. The reading should be followed by immediate checking of answers for immediate feedback.

See pages 79 and 80 for examples of the format for reading parts 1 and 2 of lesson 1–A.

To the Student

Read this page carefully before you use the lessons in this book.

This is the workbook for a series of thirty-two language laboratory lessons—*Listening Dictation: Understanding English Sentence Structure.*

USING THE LESSONS

Part 1 of each tape is called "Listen, Repeat, and Write." You will listen to the sentence, repeat it aloud (carefully imitating the rhythm and intonation pattern), listen again (to the same sentence), write the sentence, listen again, and check your answer. The numbers on the *right* side of each line tell the number of words in the sentence.

Part 2 of each tape is called "Multiple Choice." You will listen to a sentence, rapidly read the three possible answers, and circle the one answer which you believe to be correct. (The sentences you hear in part 2 of each lesson are the same sentences which you write in part 1 of the lesson. The order will be different.)

COORDINATION WITH *ENGLISH SENTENCE STRUCTURE*

There are eight units of four lessons each. The first *six* units correspond to the lessons in *English Sentence Structure*, by Robert Krohn. The remaining *two* units are review lessons. The four lessons in each unit are equal in difficulty, i.e., tape D is no more difficult than tape A. The tapes correspond to the grammar lessons as follows:

Tape	1–A		Tape	5–A	
	1–B	Grammar Lessons		5–B	Grammar Lessons
	1–C	1–5		5–C	21–25
	1–D			5–D	
Tape	2–A		Tape	6–A	
	2–B	Grammar Lessons		6–B	Grammar Lessons
	2–C	6–10		6–C	26–30
	2–D			6–D	
Tape	3–A		Tape	7–A	
	3–B	Grammar Lessons		7–B	Review–
	3–C	11–15		7–C	All Lessons
	3–D			7–D	
Tape	4–A		Tape	8–A	
	4–B	Grammar Lessons		8–B	Review–
	4–C	16–20		8–C	All Lessons
	4–D			8–D	

The last eight lessons (units 7 and 8) are review practice with patterns from all thirty grammar lessons. Each of these lessons contains twenty-five multiple choice items. (No sentence dictation is included in these lessons.) The last two tapes in each set 7–C, 7–D, 8–C, and 8–D) are done at a fast speed and are quite difficult.

THE IMPORTANCE OF SELF-CORRECTION

When you finish a lesson check your answers in the answer key. It is *very* important for you to check your answers. Circle your mistakes. Analyze your errors and discuss them with your teacher. If you have many errors on a lesson, do it a second time. Particular attention should be given to—

> suffix errors or omissions (-ed, -es, -s, -'s, -ing, -ly, -er, -est),
> function word errors or omissions (articles, prepositions, conjunctions, pronouns, auxiliaries),
> spelling, punctuation, capitalization errors.

WORKBOOK

LESSON 1—A

Part 1—Listen, Repeat, and Write: *Listen carefully. Repeat the sentence aloud. Listen again. Write the sentence. Listen again. Check your answer.*

1. _____ (4 words)

2. _____ (4)

3. _____ (3)

4. _____ (5)

5. _____ (4)

6. _____ (5)

7. _____ (5)

8. _____ (5)

9. _____ (4)

10. _____ (4)

11. _____ (7)

12. _____ (4)

13. _____ (6)

14. _____ (3)

15. _____ (8)

Part 2—Multiple Choice: *Draw a circle around the letter of the correct answer. There is only* one *best answer to each question.*

1. a. He is from Mexico.
   b. They are from Mexico.
   c. It is from Mexico.

2. a. It has it.
   b. They have it.
   c. He has it.

3. a. Yes, they do.
   b. Yes, they are.
   c. Yes, he does.

4. a. They don't drink coffee.
   b. They always drink coffee.
   c. They seldom drink coffee.

5. a. Last night.
   b. Now.
   c. Every day.

6. a. Yes, I am.
   b. Yes, I was.
   c. Yes, I did.

7. a. Yes, she is.
   b. Yes, it is.
   c. Yes, he is.

8. a. Yes, they are.
   b. Yes, I am.
   c. Yes, we are.

9. a. Yes, it is.
   b. Yes, he is.
   c. Yes, they are.

10. a. Yes, they are.
    b. Yes, it is.
    c. Yes, she is.

11. a. Yes, I do.
    b. Yes, they do.
    c. Yes, you do.

12. a. I always drink milk.
    b. I never drink milk.
    c. I often drink milk.

13. a. Bob is at home.
    b. It is twelve o'clock.
    c. Bob goes home at twelve o'clock.

14. a. Yes, he did.
    b. Yes, he is.
    c. Yes, he was.

15. a. Every day.
    b. Now.
    c. Last night.

LESSON 1—B

Part 1—Listen, Repeat, and Write: *Listen carefully. Repeat the sentence aloud. Listen again. Write the sentence. Listen again. Check your answer.*

1. _____ (4 words)

2. _____ (5)

3. _____ (7)

4. _____ (6)

5. _____ (5)*

6. _____ (6)

7. _____ (7)

8. _____ (7)

9. _____ (6)

10. _____ (6)†

11. _____ (4)

12. _____ (6)‡

13. _____ (4)

14. _____ (6)

15. _____ (3)

Part 2—Multiple Choice: *Draw a circle around the letter of the correct answer. There is only* one *best answer to each question.*

1. a. Yes, they did.
   b. In the library.
   c. Last night.

2. a. No, she isn't living.
   b. No, she isn't.
   c. No, she wasn't.

---

* One of the words in sentence 5 is a compound word (typewriter).
† One of the words in sentence 10 is a contraction.
‡ One of the words in sentence 12 is a compound word (snowboots).

3. a. Yes, he wants a spoon.
    b. Yes, he wants a cup.
    c. Yes, he wants some soup.

4. a. Yes, they did.
    b. Yesterday morning.
    c. In the library.

5. a. He is studying now.
    b. He studied yesterday.
    c. He studies every day.

6. a. Mary has.
    b. Tomorrow.
    c. Mary is.

7. a. Last night.
    b. I am.
    c. This evening.

8. a. In the morning.
    b. Wash the dishes.
    c. In the house.

9. a. They never go.
    b. They seldom go.
    c. They often go.

10. a. Yes, she is.
     b. Yes, it is.
     c. Yes, he is.

11. a. Yes, it is.
     b. Yes, he is.
     c. Yes, they are.

12. a. Tomorrow night.
     b. Yesterday evening.
     c. At the theatre.

13. a. They are going to go there.
     b. They didn't go there.
     c. They went there.

14. a. Yes, it has books.
     b. No, it has blue snowboots.
     c. Yes, it has some.

15. a. Yes, they are.
     b. Yes, I am.
     c. Yes, we are.

LESSON 1—C

Part 1—Listen, Repeat, and Write: *Listen carefully. Repeat the sentence aloud. Listen again. Write the sentence. Listen again. Check your answer.*

1. _____ (5 words)

2. _____ (4)

3. _____ (7)

4. _____ (5)

5. _____ (5)

6. _____ (4)

7. _____ (4)

8. _____ (8)

9. _____ (5)

10. _____ (5)

11. _____ (3)

12. _____ (8)

13. _____ (4)

14. _____ (5)

15. _____ (6)

Part 2—Multiple Choice: *Draw a circle around the letter of the correct answer. There is only* one *best answer to each question.*

1. a. It has it.
    b. They have it.
    c. He has it.

2. a. Yes, they do.
    b. Yes, they are.
    c. Yes, he does.

3. a. I always eat fish.
    b. I seldom eat fish.
    c. I don't eat fish.

4. a. Last night.
   b. Tomorrow.
   c. Now.

5. a. Now.
   b. Last night.
   c. Every day.

6. a. Yes, he did.
   b. This morning.
   c. In the dorm cafeteria.

7. a. He is from Japan.
   b. They are from Japan.
   c. It is from Japan.

8. a. Yes, I do.
   b. Yes, you do.
   c. Yes, they do.

9. a. Yes, they are.
   b. Yes, it is.
   c. Yes, she is.

10. a. They often eat hamburgers.
    b. They always eat hamburgers.
    c. They never eat hamburgers.

11. a. Mary went to the restaurant.
    b. Mary eats at twelve o'clock.
    c. It is twelve o'clock.

12. a. Yes, he is.
    b. Yes, he was.
    c. Yes, he did.

13. a. Yes, he did.
    b. Yes, I did.
    c. Yes, I am.

14. a. He swims every day.
    b. He swam yesterday.
    c. He is swimming now.

15. a. At home.
    b. Yes, she did.
    c. Last night.

LESSON 1—D

Part 1—Listen, Repeat, and Write: *Listen carefully. Repeat the sentence aloud. Listen again. Write the sentence. Listen again. Check your answer.*

1. _____ (5 words)

2. _____ (5)

3. _____ (6)

4. _____ (7)

5. _____ (8)

6. _____ (6)

7. _____ (6)*

8. _____ (3)

9. _____ (6)†

10. _____ (4)

Part 2—Multiple Choice: *Draw a circle around the letter of the correct answer. There is only* one *best answer to each question.*

1. a. Tomorrow night.
   b. Yesterday morning.
   c. On the bus.

2. a. Yes, it has it.
   b. Yes, it has some.
   c. No, it has blue gloves.

3. a. No, she isn't.
   b. No, she isn't living.
   c. No, she wasn't.

4. a. She never smokes.
   b. She seldom smokes.
   c. She often smokes.

5. a. Jim has.
   b. Jim is.
   c. Tomorrow.

---

* One of the words in sentence 7 is a contraction.
† One of the words in sentence 9 is a compound word (bookstore).

9

6. a. In the yard.
   b. This afternoon.
   c. Wash the car.

7. a. Yes, he wants a watch.
   b. What time is it?
   c. Yes, she wants a watch.

8. a. They went there.
   b. They are going to go there.
   c. They didn't go there.

9. a. I'm from Venezuela.
   b. She's from Venezuela.
   c. He's from Venezuela.

10. a. He is.
    b. Last night.
    c. This evening.

LESSON 2—A

Part 1–Listen, Repeat, and Write: *Listen carefully. Repeat the sentence aloud. Listen again. Write the sentence. Listen again. Check your answer.*

1. _____ (5 words)

2. _____ (5)*

3. _____ (3)

4. _____ (8)

5. _____ (6)

6. _____ (5)

7. _____ (4)

8. _____ (9)

9. _____ (11)

10. _____ (4)

11. _____

_____ (14)†

12. _____ (7)

Part 2–Multiple Choice: *Draw a circle around the letter of the correct answer. There is only* one *best answer to each question.*

1. a. It is with them.
   b. They are with them.
   c. They are with her.

2. a. Some of them went.
   b. Not any of them went.
   c. Not all of them went.

3. a. The chairs are there.
   b. The chairs are here.
   c. The chair is there.

---

* One of the words in sentence 2 is a contraction.

† One of the words in sentence 11 has an apostrophe (o'clock).

4. a. The other.
   b. The coats.
   c. The coat.

5. a. Let's buy another.
   b. Let's buy some.
   c. Let's buy them.

6. a. Some teachers are from Chicago.
   b. All the teachers are from Chicago.
   c. One teacher is from Chicago.

7. a. It's nine o'clock now.
   b. The students are at the language lab now.
   c. The students are going to go to the language lab.

8. a. I want a lot of milk.
   b. I don't want much milk.
   c. He wants a lot of milk.

9. a. That food is expensive.
   b. Some food is expensive.
   c. All food is expensive.

10. a. She is good.
    b. He is good.
    c. They are good.

11. a. Yes, she is.
    b. Yes, they are.
    c. Yes, it is cold.

12. a. I have a lot of coffee.
    b. I have a little coffee.
    c. I don't have coffee.

LESSON 2—B

Part 1—Listen, Repeat, and Write: *Listen carefully. Repeat the sentence aloud. Listen again. Write the sentence. Listen again. Check your answer.*

1. _____ (6 words)

2. _____ (8)

3. _____ (7)

4. _____ (6)

5. _____ (5)

6. _____ (5)

7. _____ (10)

8. _____ (8)

9. _____ (10)

10. _____ (5)

11. _____ (7)

12. _____ (7)

Part 2—Multiple Choice: *Draw a circle around the letter of the correct answer. There is only* one *best answer to each question.*

1. a. They gave it.
   b. She gave it.
   c. He gave it.

2. a. She corrected the answers.
   b. The questions were correct.
   c. The answers were correct.

3. a. The book is red.
   b. I lost the cover.
   c. The cover is red.

4. a. The cup is plastic.
   b. The handle is plastic.
   c. The box is plastic.

5. a. The teachers.
    b. Very often.
    c. Four teachers.

6. a. We asked the questions.
    b. They asked the questions.
    c. They answered the questions.

7. a. The students.
    b. The words.
    c. The teacher.

8. a. She thinks well.
    b. She teaches well.
    c. She talks well.

9. a. In a hurry.
    b. In the bedroom.
    c. In the morning.

10. a. John is a rapid speaker.
     b. Maria speaks rapidly.
     c. George is a rapid speaker.

11. a. He asked it.
     b. She asked it.
     c. They asked it.

12. a. He does.
     b. The lesson.
     c. The vocabulary lesson.

LESSON 2—C

Part 1—Listen, Repeat, and Write: *Listen carefully. Repeat the sentence aloud. Listen again. Write the sentence. Listen again. Check your answer.*

1. _____ (9 words)

2. _____ (6)

3. _____ (5)

4. _____ (7)

5. _____ (5)

6. _____ (4)

7. _____ (10)

8. _____ (8)

9. _____

_____ (14)*

10. _____ (7)

11. _____ (10)

12. _____ (5)†

Part 2—Multiple Choice: *Draw a circle around the letter of the correct answer. There is only* one *best answer to each question.*

1. a. He wants a lot of lunch.
   b. She wants a lot of lunch.
   c. He doesn't want much lunch.

2. a. In the evening.
   b. In the bedroom.
   c. In a hurry.

3. a. Some students went to Michigan.
   b. One student went to Michigan.
   c. All the students went to Michigan.

_____

* One of the words in sentence 9 has an apostrophe (o'clock).
† One of the words in sentence 12 is a contraction.

4. a. The children are at the swimming pool now.
    b. The children are always late.
    c. The children are going to the swimming pool.

5. a. The desk is plastic.
    b. The book is plastic.
    c. The cover is plastic.

6. a. He has a class at eight o'clock.
    b. The biology class.
    c. The class.

7. a. He has a lot of milk.
    b. He has a little milk.
    c. He doesn't have any milk.

8. a. The other.
    b. The books.
    c. The others.

9. a. They gave the directions.
    b. They got the directions.
    c. We gave the directions.

10. a. Some clothing costs a lot of money.
    b. That clothing costs a lot of money.
    c. All clothing costs a lot of money.

11. a. Yes, he is.
    b. Yes, she is.
    c. Yes, they are.

12. a. All the students went to the hockey game.
    b. They seldom go to a hockey game.
    c. The teachers went to the hockey game.

LESSON 2—D

Part 1—Listen, Repeat, and Write: *Listen carefully. Repeat the sentence aloud. Listen again. Write the sentence. Listen again. Check your answer.*

1. _____ (6 words)

2. _____ (6)

3. _____ (4)

4. _____ (4)

5. _____ (7)

6. _____ (8)

7. _____ (7)

8. _____ (5)

9. _____ (11)

10. _____ (8)

Part 2—Multiple Choice: *Draw a circle around the letter of the correct answer. There is only* one *best answer to each question.*

1. a. The pencils are here.
   b. The pencils are there.
   c. The pencil is here.

2. a. They are with them.
   b. It is with them.
   c. They are with him.

3. a. She teaches well.
   b. She thinks well.
   c. She talks well.

4. a. The book is green
   b. The box is green.
   c. The top is green.

5. a. Some of them were hurt.
   b. Not all of them were hurt.
   c. Not any of them were hurt.

6. a.   Susan is a rapid speaker.
    b.   Henry is a rapid speaker.
    c.   Bob is a rapid speaker.

7. a.   She is good.
    b.   They are good.
    c.   It is good.

8. a.   Let's buy another.
    b.   Let's buy some.
    c.   Let's buy them.

9. a.   An exercise.
    b.   The students.
    c.   Yesterday.

10. a.   I corrected the answer.
     b.   The question was correct.
     c.   The answer was correct.

LESSON 3—A

Part 1—Listen, Repeat, and Write: *Listen carefully. Repeat the sentence aloud. Listen again. Write the sentence. Listen again. Check your answer.*

1. _____ (8 words)

2. _____ (8)

3. _____ (7)*

4. _____ (8)†

5. _____ (7)‡

6. _____ (4)

7. _____ (6)

8. _____ (7)§

9. _____

_____ (15)‖

10. _____ (7)

11. _____ (8)

12. _____ (6)

13. _____ (8)

14. _____ (7)

Part 2—Multiple Choice: *Draw a circle around the letter of the correct answer. There is only* one *best answer to each question.*

1. a. She's not going to take them.
   b. She is taking them.
   c. She's going to take them.

2. a. Mary can't skate.
   b. Tom can skate.
   c. Mary can skate.

---

* One word in sentence 3 is a contraction.
† One word in sentence 4 is a contraction.
‡ Two words in sentence 5 are contractions.

§ One word in sentence 8 is a compound word (drugstore).
‖ One word in sentence 9 is a possessive form.

3. a. He woke them.
    b. He telephoned them.
    c. He waited for them.

4. a. He's going for beer.
    b. He's going for Mr. Lane.
    c. He's going for the weekend.

5. a. In the morning.
    b. For fun.
    c. By train.

6. a. They must read it.
    b. They have it.
    c. They read many of them.

7. a. Yes, please bring it to me.
    b. I don't like you.
    c. Yes, I have it.

8. a. Bob played after Mary.
    b. Bob is playing golf.
    c. Bob isn't playing golf.

9. a. Frank is swimming.
    b. John is swimming.
    c. None of them are swimming.

10. a. She visited him.
    b. He visited her.
    c. He telephoned her.

11. a. Slowly.
    b. For some toothpaste.
    c. By car.

12. a. She worked hard.
    b. Her teacher worked hard.
    c. They both worked hard.

13. a. No, but she didn't.
    b. No, but she must.
    c. No, but she had to.

14. a. In the evening.
    b. With soap and water.
    c. To look nice.

LESSON 3—B

Part 1—Listen, Repeat, and Write: *Listen carefully. Repeat the sentence aloud. Listen again. Write the sentence. Listen again. Check your answer.*

1. _____ (10 words)

2. _____ (9)

3. _____ (7)

4. _____ (10)

5. _____ (5)

6. _____ (6)*

7. _____ (5)†

8. _____ (4)

9. _____ (12)

10. _____ (7)‡

11. _____ (10)

12. _____ (11)

13. _____ (7)

14. _____ (11)

Part 2—Multiple Choice: *Draw a circle around the letter of the correct answer. There is only one best answer to each question.*

1. a. I can't learn the lesson.
   b. I can learn the lesson.
   c. I don't like the lesson.

2. a. She wants to write a letter.
   b. He wants to write a letter.
   c. He wants a letter from her.

---

* One word in sentence 6 is a contraction, and a second word in sentence 6 has an apostrophe (o'clock).
† One word in sentence 7 is a possessive form.
‡ Two words in sentence 10 are possessive forms.

3. a. A plane leaves at twelve o'clock.
   b. A plane leaves at two o'clock.
   c. The plane is over there.

4. a. This is Peter.
   b. It's Peter.
   c. It's mine.

5. a. Peter's is bigger.
   b. John's is bigger.
   c. They are the same size.

6. a. Both are good.
   b. The old one is better.
   c. The new one is better.

7. a. Both swim slowly.
   b. John swims faster than Mary.
   c. Mary swims faster than John.

8. a. She can buy it.
   b. She can't buy it.
   c. She bought it.

9. a. She learned to speak slowly.
   b. He learned to speak slowly.
   c. He taught her slowly.

10. a. She's Mary.
    b. There's Mary.
    c. It's Mary.

11. a. It's Mary.
    b. It's a girl.
    c. It's her name.

12. a. I have some shirts.
    b. He has some shirts.
    c. He has one shirt.

13. a. The little one costs more.
    b. The big one costs more.
    c. They both cost the same.

14. a. My horse is older.
    b. Our horses are the same age.
    c. Your horse is older.

LESSON 3—C

Part 1—Listen, Repeat, and Write: *Listen carefully. Repeat the sentence aloud. Listen again. Write the sentence. Listen again. Check your answer.*

1. _____ (8 words)

2. _____ (5)

3. _____ (9)

4. _____

_____ (16)*

5. _____ (4)†

6. _____ (5)‡

7. _____ (11)

8. _____ (10)

9. _____ (7)§

10. _____ (6)

11. _____ (6)//

12. _____ (11)

13. _____ (8)#

14. _____ (7)

Part 2—Multiple Choice: *Draw a circle around the letter of the correct answer. There is only* one *best answer to each question.*

1. a. She visited her.
   b. She woke her.
   c. She telephoned her.

2. a. He's going to visit Mr. Brown.
   b. He's going for a typewriter.
   c. He went last week.

---

* One word in sentence 4 is a possessive form, and a second word is a compound word (typewriter).
† One word in sentence 5 is a contraction.
‡ One word in sentence 6 is a possessive form.

§ Two words in sentence 9 are contractions.
// One word in sentence 11 is a contraction, and a second word has an apostrophe (o'clock).
One word in sentence 13 is a contraction.

23

3. a. It's a woman.
    b. It's Mrs. Brown.
    c. It's Mr. Brown.

4. a. The red book costs more.
    b. The black book costs more.
    c. They both cost the same.

5. a. In the morning.
    b. By plane.
    c. For a meeting.

6. a. The old one is better.
    b. Both are good.
    c. The new one is better.

7. a. No, but he had to.
    b. No, but he didn't.
    c. No, but he must.

8. a. Yes, I learned it yesterday.
    b. Yes, please bring it to me.
    c. I like John.

9. a. They ate it.
    b. They studied it.
    c. They must study it.

10. a. It's the teacher.
     b. She's the teacher.
     c. There's the teacher.

11. a. Bob eats faster than Betty.
     b. Betty eats faster than Bob.
     c. Both eat slowly.

12. a. Bob can drive.
     b. Susan can't drive.
     c. Susan can drive.

13. a. The bus leaves at six o'clock.
     b. The bus leaves at eight o'clock.
     c. The bus is over there.

14. a. Bob is a student.
     b. Mary is a student.
     c. None of them are students.

LESSON 3—D

Part 1—Listen, Repeat, and Write: *Listen carefully. Repeat the sentence aloud. Listen again. Write the sentence. Listen again. Check your answer.*

1. _____ (10 words)

2. _____ (4)

3. _____ (7)

4. _____ (7)*

5. _____ (10)

6. _____ (7)†

7. _____ (7)

8. _____ (12)

9. _____ (7)

10. _____ (9)

11. _____ (6)

12. _____ (8)

13. _____ (5)

14. _____ (7)

Part 2—Multiple Choice: *Draw a circle around the letter of the correct answer. There is only one best answer to each question.*

1. a. It's Mary.
   b. This is Mary.
   c. It's mine.

2. a. They are not going to go.
   b. They are going to go.
   c. They are late.

3. a. They are the same length.
   b. Mary's dress is longer.
   c. Elaine's dress is longer.

---

* One word in sentence 4 is a contraction.
† Two words in sentence 6 are possessives.

4. a. Jim has one notebook.
   b. Jim has some notebooks.
   c. Mary has some notebooks.

5. a. I like the airplane.
   b. I can fly the airplane.
   c. I can't fly the airplane.

6. a. In a minute.
   b. For a loaf of bread.
   c. Yesterday.

7. a. Mary isn't skating.
   b. Betty isn't skating.
   c. Both are skating.

8. a. He wants to write a letter.
   b. She wants to write a letter.
   c. She wants a letter from him.

9. a. They worked hard.
   b. He worked hard.
   c. She worked hard.

10. a. He can't buy it.
    b. He can buy it.
    c. He bought it.

11. a. My car is newer.
    b. His car is older.
    c. The cars are the same age.

12. a. She learned to speak softly.
    b. He learned to speak softly.
    c. She taught him to speak loudly.

13. a. With liquid polish.
    b. In the morning.
    c. In the kitchen.

14. a. The teacher telephoned John.
    b. The teacher visited John.
    c. John telephoned the teacher.

LESSON 4—A

Part 1—Listen, Repeat, and Write: *Listen carefully. Repeat the sentence aloud. Listen again. Write the sentence. Listen again. Check your answer.*

1. _____ (7 words)

2. _____ (10)

3. _____ (8)

4. _____ (8)

5. _____ (8)

6. _____ (6)

7. _____ (6)

8. _____

   _____ (13)

9. _____ (6)*

10. _____ (9)

11. _____ (8)

12. _____ (9)

Part 2—Multiple Choice: *Draw a circle around the letter of the correct answer. There is only* one *best answer to each question.*

1. a. She was swimming.
   b. He was working.
   c. They were playing tennis.

2. a. Maria visited Mrs. Smith.
   b. Mrs. Smith visited Maria.
   c. Maria visited the teacher.

3. a. Yes, I remember Mary.
   b. Mr. Brown saw her.
   c. She saw Mr. Brown.

---

* Two words in sentence 9 are contractions.

4. a. Yes, I think she'll go.
    b. Yes, I think it is.
    c. Yes, I think they'll go.

5. a. I bought the record.
    b. I remember you.
    c. I remember the title of the record.

6. a. He left there ten years ago.
    b. He is going to live there for ten years.
    c. He is living there now.

7. a. The man was rewarded.
    b. Mary was rewarded.
    c. The men were rewarded.

8. a. I called Bob.
    b. I called John.
    c. Bob called John.

9. a. I didn't see them.
    b. I saw them.
    c. They saw me.

10. a. Peter visited him.
     b. He visited Peter.
     c. George is a dentist.

11. a. I'm going home.
     b. Mr. Johnson isn't here.
     c. I'm here.

12. a. I began three years ago.
     b. I finished three years ago.
     c. I am starting now.

LESSON 4—B

Part 1—Listen, Repeat, and Write: *Listen carefully. Repeat the sentence aloud. Listen again. Write the sentence. Listen again. Check your answer.*

1. _____ (8 words)

2. _____ (11)*

3. _____ (8)

4. _____ (8)

5. _____ (10)†

6. _____ (5)‡

7. _____ (6)

8. _____ (8)§

9. _____ (7)

10. _____ (6)

11. _____ (7)

12. _____ (10)

13. _____ (8)

Part 2—Multiple Choice: *Draw a circle around the letter of the correct answer. There is only* one *best answer to each question.*

1. a. He went to the language lab.
   b. He went swimming.
   c. He went to the language lab and he went swimming.

2. a. Yes, I would have.
   b. Yes, I have.
   c. Yes, I had.

3. a. He has left already.
   b. He's still here.
   c. He isn't here yet.

---

* One word in sentence 2 is a contraction.
† One word in sentence 5 is a possessive form.
‡ One word in sentence 6 is a contraction.
§ One word in sentence 8 is a possessive form.

4. a. Bob's teacher is surprised.
    b. The student is surprised.
    c. Bob is surprised.

5. a. Mary has stopped studying grammar.
    b. Mary is going to begin studying grammar.
    c. Mary studies grammar.

6. a. She was at work.
    b. He was working.
    c. They were skiing.

7. a. I am going to study for two hours.
    b. I stopped studying for two hours.
    c. I am studying now.

8. a. No, they aren't.
    b. No, they hadn't.
    c. No, they haven't.

9. a. Peter will visit his friend.
    b. He will leave his friend.
    c. His friend will leave.

10. a. He is fascinated.
    b. His students are fascinating.
    c. His students are fascinated.

11. a. I was interesting.
    b. He was interested.
    c. I was interested.

12. a. The girl was crying.
    b. John was crying.
    c. The girls were crying.

13. a. I visited Mary.
    b. I visited John.
    c. John visited Mary.

LESSON 4—C

Part 1—Listen, Repeat, and Write: *Listen carefully. Repeat the sentence aloud. Listen again. Write the sentence. Listen again. Check your answer.*

1. _____ (8 words)

2. _____ (7)

3. _____ (6)

4. _____ (6)

5. _____
   _____ (13)

6. _____ (6)*

7. _____ (9)

8. _____ (8)

9. _____ (9)

10. _____ (9)†

11. _____ (10)‡

12. _____ (7)

Part 2—Multiple Choice: *Draw a circle around the letter of the correct answer. There is only* one *best answer to each question.*

1. a. I didn't meet them.
   b. I met them.
   c. They met me.

2. a. Mary called him.
   b. He called Mary.
   c. He called his mother.

3. a. She's not here.
   b. Mr. Borman isn't here.
   c. She's here.

---

* Two words in sentence 6 are contractions.
† One word in sentence 10 is an abbreviated form (TV).
‡ One word in sentence 11 is a contraction.

4. a. I began one year ago.
    b. I finished one year ago.
    c. I am beginning now.

5. a. She is going to watch for half an hour.
    b. She stopped watching for half an hour.
    c. She is watching now.

6. a. No, they aren't.
    b. No, they hadn't.
    c. No, they haven't.

7. a. Bob telephoned the teacher.
    b. The teacher telephoned him.
    c. Mrs. Walker telephoned Bob.

8. a. Yes, I remember Bob.
    b. Mr. Johnson telephoned him.
    c. He telephoned Mr. Johnson.

9. a. Yes, I think I'll go.
    b. Yes, I think she will go.
    c. Yes, I think they'll go.

10. a. I saw the movie.
     b. I remember you.
     c. I remember the title of the movie.

11. a. She left there five years ago.
     b. She is going to live there for five years.
     c. She is living there now.

12. a. He went to the store.
     b. He went skiiing.
     c. He went to the store and he went skiing.

LESSON 4—D

Part 1—Listen, Repeat, and Write: *Listen carefully. Repeat the sentence aloud. Listen again. Write the sentence. Listen again. Check your answer.*

1. _____ (10 words)

2. _____ (10)*

3. _____ (8)†

4. _____ (6)

5. _____ (8)‡

6. _____ (7)

7. _____ (6)

8. _____ (10)

9. _____ (7)

10. _____ (7)

11. _____ (7)§

12. _____ (6)

13. _____ (8)

Part 2—Multiple Choice: *Draw a circle around the letter of the correct answer. There is only one best answer to each question.*

1. a. John will visit his brother.
   b. He will leave his brother.
   c. His brother will leave John.

2. a. He's bored.
   b. His students are boring.
   c. His students are bored.

3. a. I was frightened.
   b. The animal was frightened.
   c. I was frightening.

---

* One word in sentence 2 is a possessive form.
† One word in sentence 3 is a contraction.
‡ One word in sentence 5 is a possessive form.
§ One word in sentence 11 is a contraction.

4. a. She was writing letters.
    b. They were writing letters.
    c. He was skating.

5. a. I was inspiring.
    b. I was inspired.
    c. The speaker was tired.

6. a. Bob has stopped drinking coffee.
    b. Bob is going to begin drinking coffee.
    c. Bob drinks coffee.

7. a. Yes, I would have.
    b. Yes, I have.
    c. Yes, I had.

8. a. They have left already.
    b. They're still here.
    c. They aren't here yet.

9. a. Betty's teacher is surprised.
    b. Betty is surprised.
    c. Everybody went to lunch.

10. a. Bob has stopped smoking cigars.
    b. Bob is going to begin smoking cigars.
    c. Bob smokes cigars.

11. a. Bob visited the girl.
    b. The girl visited Bob.
    c. Helen visited Bob.

12. a. He has left already.
    b. He's still here.
    c. He isn't here yet.

13. a. The boy was laughing.
    b. The teacher was laughing.
    c. The boys were laughing.

LESSON 5—A

Part 1—Listen, Repeat, and Write: *Listen carefully. Repeat the sentence aloud. Listen again. Write the sentence. Listen again. Check your answer.*

1. _____ (9 words)

2. _____ (6)

3. _____ (8)

4. _____ (8)

5. _____ (10)*

6. _____ (5)

7. _____ (8)

8. _____ (8)

9. _____ (8)

10. _____ (9)†

11. _____
    _____ (14)‡

12. _____
    _____ (13)§

13. _____ (9)

14. _____ (10)‖

Part 2—Multiple Choice: *Draw a circle around the letter of the correct answer. There is only one best answer to each question.*

1. a. He can fly.
   b. He could fly.
   c. He can't fly.

---

* One word in sentence 5 is a compound word (shoestore).
† One word in sentence 10 is a compound word (notebook).
‡ One word in sentence 11 is a contraction.
§ One word in sentence 12 has an apostrophe (o'clock).
‖ One word in sentence 14 is an abbreviation (TV).

2. a. Mary told me where it is.
   b. I know where it is.
   c. Mary knows where it is.

3. a. She will get her husband.
   b. She got her husband.
   c. She didn't get her husband.

4. a. Yes, we should.
   b. Yes, we should have.
   c. Yes, we did.

5. a. I wasn't thinking.
   b. I was thinking.
   c. I have to think.

6. a. She talked until it began.
   b. She talked after it began.
   c. She talked because it began.

7. a. They must listen.
   b. They may listen.
   c. They don't listen.

8. a. You must study grammar.
   b. John must study.
   c. They must study grammar.

9. a. I asked him to fix my car.
   b. He wants to fix my car.
   c. I want to fix my car.

10. a. I can speak Spanish.
    b. I cannot speak Spanish.
    c. I spoke Spanish.

11. a. Yes, I might.
    b. Yes, I might have.
    c. Yes, I might be.

12. a. He didn't bring it.
    b. He brought it.
    c. He forgot his pencil.

13. a. I always go to bed at twelve o'clock.
    b. I always watch the television movie.
    c. I sometimes go to bed after twelve o'clock.

14. a. I always watch TV.
    b. I watch unless the show is bad.
    c. I watch because the shows are bad.

LESSON 5—B

Part 1—Listen, Repeat, and Write: *Listen carefully. Repeat the sentence aloud. Listen again. Write the sentence. Listen again. Check your answer.*

1. _____ (11 words)

2. _____ (11)*

3. _____ (7)†

4. _____ (13)

5. _____ (12)

6. _____
   _____ (13)

7. _____ (12)

8. _____
   _____ (15)‡

9. _____ (12)

10. _____ (11)§

11. _____ (12)‖

12. _____ (10)

13. _____ (12)#

14. _____
    _____ (14)**

15. _____
    _____ (12)††

---

*   Two words in sentence 2 are contractions.
†   One word in sentence 3 is a contraction.
‡   One word in sentence 8 is a compound (homework).
§   One word in sentence 10 is a contraction.
‖   One word in sentence 11 is a contraction.
One word in sentence 13 is a contraction.
** One word in sentence 14 is a contraction, and one word has an apostrophe (o'clock).
†† One word in sentence 15 is a contraction, and one word is a compound (drugstores).

37

Part 2–Multiple Choice: *Draw a circle around the letter of the correct answer. There is only* one *best answer to each question.*

1. a. Los Angeles is near.
   b. I'm going far away.
   c. I'm not going to go to Los Angeles.

2. a. Susan went to New York by plane.
   b. Susan has gone to New York.
   c. Susan might go to New York.

3. a. Mary stayed for dinner.
   b. We didn't ask Mary to stay for dinner.
   c. We asked Mary to stay for dinner.

4. a. He will go.
   b. He may go.
   c. He won't go.

5. a. I spend too much on clothes.
   b. I have too many clothes.
   c. I am too poor to buy many clothes.

6. a. Sam is helping him.
   b. Sam ought to help him.
   c. Sam is busy.

7. a. They can.
   b. They can't.
   c. They should.

8. a. They went although it was cold.
   b. They went because of the weather.
   c. It was too cold to go.

9. a. In spite of my test tomorrow.
   b. Because of my test tomorrow.
   c. Unless I have a test tomorrow.

10. a. He is here now.
    b. He caught the plane.
    c. He didn't catch the plane.

11. a. I got a new dress.
    b. I didn't go to the party.
    c. I need a new dress.

12. a. Betty didn't cash a check.
    b. Betty cashed a check.
    c. I cashed a check.

13. a. Betty could go by bus.
     b. Betty couldn't go by bus.
     c. Betty went by bus.

14. a. It is Mary's.
     b. It is Betty's.
     c. It isn't Betty's.

15. a. They don't sell them.
     b. They sold them.
     c. They sell them.

LESSON 5—C

Part 1—Listen, Repeat, and Write: *Listen carefully. Repeat the sentence aloud. Listen again. Write the sentence. Listen again. Check your answer.*

1. _____ (7 words)

2. _____ (6)

3. _____ (8)

4. _____ (8)

5. _____ (12)

6. _____ (5)

7. _____ (6)

8. _____ (8)

9. _____ (7)

10. _____ (9)

11. _____

    _____ (14)*

12. _____ (12)†

13. _____ (9)

14. _____ (12)

Part 2—Multiple Choice: *Draw a circle around the letter of the correct answer. There is only* one *best answer to each question.*

1. a. You must take baths.
   b. We must take baths.
   c. They must take baths.

2. a. I asked her to cook the meat.
   b. She wants to cook the meat.
   c. I want to cook the meat.

---

* One word in sentence 11 is a contraction.
† One word in sentence 12 has an apostrophe (o'clock).

3. a. She can speak Italian.
    b. She cannot speak Italian.
    c. She spoke Italian.

4. a. Yes, he might.
    b. Yes, he might have.
    c. Yes, he might be.

5. a. She didn't bring it.
    b. She brought it.
    c. She didn't go to school.

6. a. I always go to bed at ten o'clock.
    b. I always visit friends.
    c. I sometimes go to bed after ten o'clock.

7. a. He always eats at the Union.
    b. He eats at the Union unless the food is bad.
    c. He eats at the Union because the food is bad.

8. a. I must drive the car.
    b. I may drive the car.
    c. I don't drive the car.

9. a. She can ride.
    b. She could ride.
    c. She can't ride.

10. a. Bob told me where it is.
     b. I know where it is.
     c. Bob knows where it is.

11. a. She will get her cleaning.
     b. She got her cleaning.
     c. She didn't get her cleaning.

12. a. Yes, we should.
     b. Yes, we should have.
     c. Yes, we studied.

13. a. I wasn't thinking.
     b. I was thinking.
     c. I have to think.

14. a. He studied until it began.
     b. He studied after it began.
     c. He studied because it began.

LESSON 5—D

Part 1—Listen, Repeat, and Write: *Listen carefully. Repeat the sentence aloud. Listen again. Write the sentence. Listen again. Check your answer.*

1. _____ (11 words)

2. _____ (10)*

3. _____ (7)†

4. _____ (12)

5. _____
   _____ (13)

6. _____ (11)

7. _____ (12)

8. _____
   _____ (16)

9. _____ (12)

10. _____ (11)‡

11. _____ (12)§

12. _____ (12)∥

13. _____ (10)

14. _____
    _____ (14)#

15. _____
    _____ (13)**

---

* Two words in sentence 2 are contractions.
† One word in sentence 3 is a contraction.
‡ One word in sentence 10 is a contraction.
§ One word in sentence 11 is a contraction.
∥ One word in sentence 12 is a contraction.
One word in sentence 14 is a contraction, and one word has an apostrophe (o'clock).
** One word in sentence 15 is a contraction, and one word is a compound (notebooks).

Part 2—Multiple Choice: *Draw a circle around the letter of the correct answer. There is only* one *best answer to each question.*

1. a. In spite of my test tomorrow.
    b. Because of my examination tomorrow.
    c. Unless I have a test tomorrow.

2. a. She is here now.
    b. She caught the train.
    c. She didn't catch the train.

3. a. He got a new suit.
    b. He didn't go to the dance.
    c. He needs a new suit.

4. a. Frank didn't return my book.
    b. Frank returned my book.
    c. I returned a book.

5. a. Betty could go by train.
    b. Betty went by train.
    c. Betty couldn't go by train.

6. a. Mary is helping her.
    b. Mary ought to help her.
    c. Mary is busy.

7. a. They don't sell them.
    b. They sold them.
    c. They sell them.

8. a. He went although it was dangerous.
    b. He went because of the riots.
    c. It was too dangerous to go.

9. a. Tokyo is near.
    b. He's going far away.
    c. He's not going to go to Tokyo.

10. a. Bob went to Detroit by train.
     b. Bob has gone to Detroit.
     c. Bob might go to Detroit.

11. a. Frank stayed for lunch.
     b. We didn't ask Frank to stay for lunch.
     c. We asked Frank to stay for lunch.

12. a. She will go.
     b. She may go.
     c. She won't go.

13. a. They spend too much on movies.
    b. They see too many movies.
    c. They are too poor to see many movies.

14. a. They are Bob's.
    b. They are Frank's.
    c. They aren't Frank's.

15. a. They can.
    b. They can't.
    c. They shouldn't.

LESSON 6—A

Part 1—Listen, Repeat, and Write: *Listen carefully. Repeat the sentence aloud. Listen again. Write the sentence. Listen again. Check your answer.*

1. _____ (8 words)

2. _____ (12)

3. _____ (6)

4. _____ (11)*

5. _____ (10)

6. _____ (6)

7. _____ (5)

8. _____ (8)

9. _____ (10)

10. _____ (5)

11. _____ (10)

Part 2—Multiple Choice: *Draw a circle around the letter of the correct answer. There is only one best answer to each question.*

1. a. He is eating.
   b. He is finished.
   c. He kept it.

2. a. Mary's mother is making a hat for Mary.
   b. Mary is making a hat for herself.
   c. Mary's mother is making a hat for herself.

3. a. He was frightened.
   b. The animals were frightened.
   c. He found several animals.

4. a. Bob read about a French university.
   b. Bob is going to a French university.
   c. Bob described life at a French university.

_____
* One word in sentence 4 is a possessive form.

5. a. Mr. Lane was ice skating with the boys.
    b. The boys were watching Mr. Lane.
    c. Mr. Lane was watching the boys ice skating.

6. a. I'm looking for the water.
    b. I'm looking at the water myself.
    c. I'm looking at myself in the water.

7. a. Bob likes to wash the car.
    b. Bob's father likes to wash the car.
    c. Bob doesn't wash the car.

8. a. The secretary typed John's paper.
    b. John typed his own paper.
    c. Betty typed her own paper.

9. a. Kennedy elected them.
    b. Kennedy selected the people.
    c. The people chose Kennedy.

10. a. I want a clean watch.
    b. I want it cleaned.
    c. I want to clean it.

11. a. The president is the secretary.
    b. Betty is the secretary.
    c. Betty chose the secretary.

LESSON 6—B

Part 1—Listen, Repeat, and Write: *Listen carefully. Repeat the sentence aloud. Listen again. Write the sentence. Listen again. Check your answer.*

1. _____ (10 words)

2. _____ (10)

3. _____ (10)

4. _____ (10)

5. _____

   _____ (15)

6. _____ (11)*

7. _____

   _____ (14)

8. _____

   _____

   _____ (27)

9. _____

   _____ (18)

10. _____ (10)

Part 2—Multiple Choice: *Draw a circle around the letter of the correct answer. There is only* one *best answer to each question.*

1. a. Mary bought a present for John.
   b. John went home early.
   c. John bought a present for Mary.

2. a. She was going to the office.
   b. He was going to the office.
   c. She found him.

3. a. My parents are going to visit me.
   b. I am going to go swimming.
   c. My parents are going swimming.

---
* One word in sentence 6 is a contraction.

4. a. However, he worked five hours.
   b. In other words, he worked five hours.
   c. So, he worked until five o'clock.

5. a. He's a good pilot but he flies rather fast.
   b. He flies too fast.
   c. He doesn't fly well.

6. a. Bill was tired Wednesday night.
   b. Bill studied Wednesday night.
   c. Bill studied on Thursday.

7. a. She didn't watch TV.
   b. She didn't do her homework.
   c. She watched TV after she finished her homework.

8. a. The class explained the word.
   b. The student explained the word.
   c. The student wrote the explanation.

9. a. First, she washed her hair.
   b. First, she studied.
   c. First, she called John.

10. a. They visited New York after Washington.
    b. They visited Washington after Miami.
    c. They visited Miami after New York.

LESSON 6—C

Part 1—Listen, Repeat, and Write: *Listen carefully. Repeat the sentence aloud. Listen again. Write the sentence. Listen again. Check your answer.*

1. _____ (9 words)

2. _____ (12)

3. _____ (7)

4. _____ (10)*

5. _____ (10)

6. _____ (6)

7. _____ (5)

8. _____ (8)

9. _____ (10)

10. _____ (5)

11. _____ (9)

Part 2—Multiple Choice: *Draw a circle around the letter of the correct answer. There is only* one *best answer to each question.*

1. a. He is finished.
   b. He is working.
   c. He kept it.

2. a. Bob is building a desk for himself.
   b. Bob's father is building a desk for himself.
   c. Bob's father is building a desk for Bob.

3. a. The snakes were frightened.
   b. He found several snakes.
   c. He was frightened.

4. a. Mary described life at a British college.
   b. Mary is going to a British college.
   c. Mary read about a British college.

_____

* One word in sentence 4 is a possessive form.

5. a. The girls were watching Mrs. Smith.
   b. Mrs. Smith was watching the girls swimming.
   c. Mrs. Smith was swimming with the girls.

6. a. He's looking at the water himself.
   b. He's looking at himself in the water.
   c. He's looking for the water.

7. a. Mary doesn't sweep the floor.
   b. Mary likes to sweep the floor.
   c. Mary's mother likes to sweep the floor.

8. a. Mary typed her own letter.
   b. Someone typed Bill's letter.
   c. Bill typed his own letter.

9. a. The students chose John.
   b. John selected the students.
   c. John elected them.

10. a. I want it fixed.
    b. I want to fix it.
    c. I want a car.

11. a. The dictator is the treasurer.
    b. John chose the treasurer.
    c. John is the treasurer.

LESSON 6—D

Part 1—Listen, Repeat, and Write: *Listen carefully. Repeat the sentence aloud. Listen again. Write the sentence. Listen again. Check your answer.*

1. _____ (10 words)

2. _____ (10)

3. _____ (10)

4. _____ (10)

5. _____ (11)*

6. _____

   _____ (15)

7. _____

   _____ (14)

8. _____

   _____

   _____ (26)

9. _____

   _____ (18)

10. _____ (9)

Part 2—Multiple Choice: *Draw a circle around the letter of the correct answer. There is only* one *best answer to each question.*

1. a. Bob went home early.
    b. Dick bought a shirt for Bob.
    c. Bob bought a shirt for Dick.

2. a. He found her.
    b. He found the library.
    c. She was going to the library.

_____

* One word in sentence 5 is a contraction.

3. a. The teacher wrote the explanation.
    b. The students explained the word.
    c. The teacher explained the word.

4. a. So, she worked until four o'clock.
    b. However, she worked four hours.
    c. In other words, she worked four hours.

5. a. He's a good rider although he rides rather fast.
    b. He rides too fast.
    c. He isn't a good rider.

6. a. Dick worked Friday night.
    b. Dick was tired Friday night.
    c. Dick worked on Saturday.

7. a. He played volleyball after he finished his homework.
    b. He didn't play volleyball.
    c. He didn't do his homework.

8. a. My brother is playing volleyball.
    b. My brother is going to visit us.
    c. I am going to play volleyball.

9. a. First, he called Mary.
    b. First, he took a bath.
    c. First, he read a book.

10. a. They visited Tokyo after Honolulu.
    b. They visited Honolulu after Los Angeles.
    c. They visited Los Angeles after Tokyo.

LESSON 7—A

Multiple Choice: *Listen carefully. Choose one answer. Draw a circle around the letter. There will be twelve seconds between the sentences. Ready? Begin.*

1. a. She saw the movie.
    b. She wants to see the movie.
    c. She likes the movie.

2. a. Mary likes the lesson.
    b. The lesson is hard.
    c. Mary does the lesson easily.

3. a. We visited her.
    b. She visited us.
    c. We were too busy.

4. a. Children eat food.
    b. They must eat nutritious food.
    c. They won't eat it.

5. a. They were interesting.
    b. He was interesting.
    c. He was interested.

6. a. Mary has two cars.
    b. Mary has three dresses.
    c. Mary has four dresses.

7. a. Sam works for Jim.
    b. Jim is a fast worker.
    c. Jim likes Sam.

8. a. The classes are easy.
    b. Sally studies hard.
    c. The classes are hard.

9. a. She went with her mother.
    b. She went by train.
    c. She went in order to buy a new coat.

10. a. Susan saw her teacher.
    b. Susan visited her teacher.
    c. Susan telephoned her teacher.

11. a. Fred will write to me. Bob won't write.
    b. Bob and Fred will write to me.
    c. Bob will write to me. Fred won't write.

12. a. Mary might go.
    b. Mary should stay.
    c. Mary has to leave.

13. a. The teacher expected us to pass the test.
    b. The teacher passed the test.
    c. The teacher didn't expect us to pass the test.

14. a. The coat is the right size for Susan.
    b. The coat is the right size for Judy.
    c. The coat is the right size for Judy and Susan.

15. a. The teacher sings the songs.
    b. The students sing the songs.
    c. No one sings the songs.

16. a. The teachers speak English easily.
    b. English is easy.
    c. Teaching English is hard.

17. a. My book is in the closet.
    b. Whose book is in the closet?
    c. The book is not in the closet.

18. a. The wall was blue.
    b. The picture was blue.
    c. The picture and the wall were both blue.

19. a. John is taller than Peter.
    b. They are the same height.
    c. Peter is taller than John.

20. a. He learned in Spain.
    b. He learned by practicing every day.
    c. He learned in order to study in Mexico.

21. a. He went for the meeting.
    b. He went yesterday.
    c. He went by bus.

22. a. Frank ran to the language lab.
    b. Bob ran to the language lab.
    c. Frank met Bob at the language lab.

23. a. Susan can sing.
    b. Bill can sing. Susan can't.
    c. Bill can't sing.

24. a. Mary works hard.
    b. Jim works hard.
    c. Mary and Jim work hard.

25. a. Jim went to the meeting.
    b. Jim is at the meeting.
    c. Jim is going to go to the meeting.

LESSON 7—B

Multiple Choice: *Listen carefully. Choose one answer. Draw a circle around the letter. There will be twelve seconds between the sentences. Ready? Begin.*

1. a. She probably finished the course.
    b. She probably didn't finish the course.
    c. She probably wants me to finish the course.

2. a. Jim visited his friends.
    b. Jim visited his friends and studied.
    c. Jim studied.

3. a. Mary found her cat.
    b. Mary isn't looking for her cat now.
    c. Mary is still looking for her cat.

4. a. Betty won't study French any more.
    b. Betty is studying French.
    c. Betty had studied French.

5. a. They are needed to finish the job.
    b. They need us.
    c. The job is finished.

6. a. They never went to the lab.
    b. They used to go to the lab.
    c. They go to the lab now.

7. a. The movie was funny.
    b. Jane was frightening.
    c. Jane was frightened.

8. a. Susan's father played chess with her mother.
    b. Susan remembers her father.
    c. Susan's father will play chess with her mother.

9. a. They studied until dinner.
    b. They studied before dinner.
    c. They studied for three hours.

10. a. Peter swam before he went to the library.
    b. Peter did not go to the library.
    c. Peter and John went to the library.

11. a. We were interested.
    b. The concert was last week.
    c. Last night was interesting.

56

12. a. Betty did not leave.
    b. Bob left the lab after Betty did.
    c. Betty left the lab last.

13. a. They are working now.
    b. They will work for six hours.
    c. They stopped working six hours ago.

14. a. She bought the dress when she had enough money.
    b. She plans to buy the dress.
    c. She didn't buy the dress.

15. a. Jim is coming to the university.
    b. Mary saw Jim.
    c. Jim has come to the university.

16. a. Nobody explained the story.
    b. Mary and Jack explained the story yesterday.
    c. Somebody explained the story yesterday.

17. a. They are going to eat lunch.
    b. They ate lunch.
    c. They are not going to eat lunch.

18. a. Bill never drinks coffee.
    b. Bill doesn't drink coffee anymore.
    c. Bill still drinks coffee.

19. a. Sam wanted the tie.
    b. Bob forgot the tie.
    c. Bob wanted the tie.

20. a. No, he isn't; he is handsome.
    b. They are all handsome.
    c. Yes, I do. The new one is the most intelligent.

21. a. The student spoke to my brother.
    b. Mary spoke to my brother.
    c. Mary knows my brother.

22. a. Fred left at eleven o'clock.
    b. Fred left at ten o'clock.
    c. Fred left at nine o'clock.

23. a. The pretty girl is always smiling.
    b. I am always smiling.
    c. We are always smiling.

24. a. Jane and Sally are more beautiful than Mary.
    b. Mary is more beautiful than Jane or Sally.
    c. Jane and Sally aren't beautiful.

25. a. Jane went to class before John.
    b. John went to class before Jane.
    c. John and Jane went to class together.

LESSON 7—C

Multiple Choice: *Listen carefully. Choose one answer. Draw a circle around the letter. There will be ten seconds between the sentences. Ready? Begin.*

1. a. Bill is going to go to the bookstore.
    b. Bill needs more books.
    c. Bill is going to need more books.

2. a. His father wanted him to go to the movies.
    b. His father didn't want him to go to the movies.
    c. His father went to the movies with him.

3. a. He is going to study the lessons.
    b. He doesn't need to study the lessons.
    c. He needs to study the lessons.

4. a. Mr. Brown may go to work today.
    b. Mr. Brown went to work today.
    c. Mr. Brown is going to work today.

5. a. Peter will probably buy the tickets at the game.
    b. Peter probably has bought the tickets already.
    c. Peter probably has to get the tickets pretty soon.

6. a. Mr. Brown walked to work because his car wouldn't start.
    b. Mr. Brown walked to work because it was a nice day.
    c. Mr. Brown drove to work because it was too nice to walk.

7. a. John believes that Mary will play this for us.
    b. John doesn't think Mary will play this for us.
    c. John can't get Mary to play this for us.

8. a. Yes, he should.
    b. Yes, he does.
    c. Yes, he should have.

9. a. I know the girls were studying.
    b. The girls have to study.
    c. I think the girls were studying.

10. a. Susan needs bread.
    b. Susan bought bread.
    c. Susan has bread.

11. a. The teacher told us to buy the tickets.
    b. We told the teacher where to buy the tickets.
    c. We know where to buy the tickets.

12. a. John can't speak English at all.
    b. John can't speak English well.
    c. John speaks English perfectly.

13. a. Professor Wilson studies very hard.
    b. They study very hard.
    c. The lessons are hard.

14. a. Peter will go to the lab if he doesn't have to work.
    b. Peter will go to the lab after he works.
    c. Peter will go to the lab if he works.

15. a. Betty stays home if it rains.
    b. It rains whenever Betty stays home.
    c. Betty drives to work if it rains.

16. a. Jim is going to New York.
    b. Jim went to New York.
    c. Jim may go to New York.

17. a. She called me.
    b. She didn't call me.
    c. I called her.

18. a. Fred asked Bill to call him.
    b. Bill asked Fred to call him.
    c. Bill didn't ask Fred to call him.

19. a. We went on a picnic because the weather was so nice.
    b. We didn't go on a picnic because of the weather.
    c. We didn't go on a picnic because of the rain.

20. a. Jim wants to finish the work before his father comes home.
    b. Jim didn't finish the work before his father came home.
    c. Jim can finish the work before his father comes home.

21. a. Yes, he did.
    b. Yes, he is.
    c. Yes, he should have.

22. a. He didn't look for the book.
    b. He found the book
    c. He saw the book this morning.

23. a. Mary knows how to ride a bicycle.
    b. Mary forgot the bicycle.
    c. Mary used to ride a bicycle.

24. a. The students can't speak French.
     b. The students want to learn English.
     c. The students speak English.

25. a. He spoke correctly.
     b. His teacher has to speak correctly.
     c. His teacher spoke correctly to him.

LESSON 7—D

Multiple Choice: *Listen carefully. Choose one answer. Draw a circle around the letter. There will be ten seconds between the sentences. Ready? Begin.*

1. a. She goes to church with Mary.
   b. She plays the piano at church.
   c. She is going to play the piano for Mary.

2. a. The man worked quickly.
   b. The beautiful girl worked quickly.
   c. The poem was beautiful.

3. a. Jim hopes he will sell his first book.
   b. Jim didn't sell his first book.
   c. Jim sold his first book.

4. a. It is easier to speak Russian than to read it or write it.
   b. It is harder to speak Russian than to read it or write it.
   c. It is difficult to learn to speak, read, and write Russian.

5. a. The meeting will be at 7:30.
   b. The breakfast will be later.
   c. There is going to be a meeting after breakfast.

6. a. Mary seldom comes to class.
   b. Mary is a poor student because she never does her work.
   c. Mary is not very intelligent.

7. a. Betty forgot to tell the student to stand by the door.
   b. Betty forgot to stand by the door.
   c. Betty forgot the student's name.

8. a. The detective's car stopped.
   b. The truck didn't stop.
   c. Someone stopped the truck for the detective.

9. a. The dog's name is Peter.
   b. The dog's name is Buster.
   c. Peter waited for the dog to come.

10. a. They studied their lessons all afternoon.
    b. They studied their lessons all evening.
    c. They didn't study their lessons.

11. a. He asked Bob to fix the car.
    b. We fixed the car ourselves.
    c. He began to fix the car.

12. a. No, she doesn't work here anymore.
    b. Yes, she does.
    c. Yes, I do.

13. a. I think John and Frank are thirsty.
    b. I don't think John and Frank are thirsty.
    c. John and Frank are hungry.

14. a. Written songs are fun.
    b. It is fun to write stories.
    c. It is fun to write songs.

15. a. He worked at the hospital because he was tired.
    b. He was tired because he had worked all day at the hospital.
    c. He was tired all day.

16. a. I stopped him.
    b. I stopped the policeman.
    c. I didn't stop him.

17. a. Bob practices every day even though he is a good swimmer.
    b. In order to become a better swimmer he practices every day.
    c. Bob is a good swimmer.

18. a. My parents are going to London before they fly to Paris.
    b. My parents are going to Montreal after they go to London.
    c. My parents are going to Paris before they go to Montreal.

19. a. Skiing is never a good idea.
    b. I like to ski alone.
    c. A person should not ski alone.

20. a. The young girls elected the secretary.
    b. Our secretary is very young.
    c. We are very young.

21. a. He worked after he went to the lecture.
    b. He worked during the lecture.
    c. He worked before he went to the lecture.

22. a. Jim wanted Mary to carry the books.
    b. Jim didn't want to go to the lab.
    c. He wanted to carry the books to the lab.

23. a. Billy watched himself.
    b. Billy's father shaved Billy.
    c. The father was shaving while Billy watched.

24. a. No, I won't go to see the movie.
    b. No, I haven't explained to the teacher yet.
    c. No, the teacher hasn't explained to me yet.

25. a. He painted the house green.
    b. The policeman has a green house.
    c. He wants someone to paint his house.

LESSON 8—A

Multiple Choice: *Listen carefully. Choose one answer. Draw a circle around the letter. There will be ten seconds between the sentences. Ready? Begin.*

1. a. He wants to see the doctor.
    b. He sees the doctor.
    c. He likes the doctor.

2. a. John likes the job.
    b. John does the job easily.
    c. The job is finished.

3. a. The Andersons visited us.
    b. The Andersons were very busy.
    c. We visited the Andersons.

4. a. Teaching English is easy.
    b. John must learn English.
    c. They must learn English.

5. a. Mary is interesting.
    b. Mary is interested.
    c. The pictures were interesting.

6. a. The millionaire has two cars.
    b. The millionaire has four cars.
    c. The millionaire has three cars.

7. a. Mr. Brown is a bad driver.
    b. Mrs. Brown likes Mr. Brown.
    c. Mrs. Brown is a good driver.

8. a. The work is difficult.
    b. The boss works hard.
    c. Mr. Smith works hard.

9. a. He went to New York last week.
    b. He went to Spain in order to learn Spanish.
    c. He went by plane.

10. a. Jim visited his girl friend.
    b. Jim telephoned his girl friend.
    c. Jim will telephone his girl friend.

11. a. My mother and my father will write to me.
    b. My mother will write to me. My father won't write.
    c. My father will write to me. My mother won't write.

12. a. Betty must leave.
    b. Betty might leave.
    c. Betty should stay.

13. a. I expect to miss the bus.
    b. My father expected me to miss the bus.
    c. My father didn't expect me to miss the bus.

14. a. The house was the right size for the Smiths.
    b. The house was not the right size for either family.
    c. The house was the right size for the Andersons.

15. a. The team doesn't learn the plays.
    b. The coach learns the plays.
    c. The team learns the plays.

16. a. Teaching languages is easy.
    b. Learning languages is hard.
    c. Children learn languages easily.

17. a. I am at home.
    b. My notebook is at home.
    c. Your notebook is at home.

18. a. The cover was green.
    b. The box and the cover were green.
    c. The box was green.

19. a. Mary is as old as Jane.
    b. Mary and Jane aren't in the same class.
    c. Mary is younger than Jane.

20. a. I learned to play the violin in Vienna.
    b. I learned to play the violin in order to play in the orchestra.
    c. I learned to play the violin by practicing every day.

21. a. He went to New York last week.
    b. He went to New York to attend the meeting.
    c. He went to New York by train.

22. a. Sam met Bill on the way to the library.
    b. Bill ran to the library.
    c. Sam ran to the library.

23. a. Mary can play the piano.
    b. I can play the piano.
    c. Mary can't play the piano.

24. a. Frank swims well.
     b. John swims well.
     c. John and Frank swim well.

25. a. Bob went to the lab.
     b. Bob is at the lab.
     c. Bob is going to go to the lab.

LESSON 8—B

Multiple Choice: *Listen carefully. Choose one answer. Draw a circle around the letter. There will be ten seconds between the sentences. Ready? Begin.*

1. a. My mother probably finished her dinner.
    b. My mother probably wants me to finish my dinner.
    c. My mother probably didn't finish her dinner.

2. a. We drove to Detroit.
    b. We worked and we drove to Detroit.
    c. We worked.

3. a. Jim found his tennis racket.
    b. Jim is still looking for his tennis racket.
    c. Jim forgot his tennis racket.

4. a. Bob had studied medicine.
    b. Bob is studying medicine.
    c. Bob won't study medicine anymore.

5. a. Their typing is finished.
    b. We need Mary and Susan.
    c. I will finish the typing.

6. a. Mr. Smith never went to the movies.
    b. Mr. Smith goes to the movies now.
    c. Mr. Smith used to go to the movies.

7. a. The students were bored.
    b. The students were boring.
    c. Professor Brown gave a lecture.

8. a. Bill played golf with his father.
    b. Bill will play golf with his father.
    c. Peter remembers his father.

9. a. Mr. Anderson and his secretary worked before lunch.
    b. Mr. Anderson and his secretary worked during lunch.
    c. Mr. Anderson and his secretary worked after lunch.

10. a. Mrs. Brown and her husband went to the store.
    b. Her husband worked before he went to the store.
    c. Her husband did not go to the store.

11. a. The football game was on Sunday.
    b. The football game was exciting.
    c. We won the football game.

12. a. Mrs. Smith did not leave.
    b. Mr. Smith did not leave.
    c. Mr. Smith left before Mrs. Smith did.

13. a. We stopped studying for four hours.
    b. We are studying now.
    c. We will study for four hours tomorrow.

14. a. Mr. Brown bought a new car.
    b. Mr. Brown didn't buy a new car.
    c. Mr. Brown will buy a new car when he gets enough money.

15. a. Mary is coming to the ELI.
    b. Maria has come to the ELI.
    c. Maria isn't at the ELI.

16. a. The exercise is hard.
    b. The students explained the exercise yesterday.
    c. Somebody explained the exercise yesterday.

17. a. She did her homework.
    b. She is going to do her homework.
    c. She is not going to do her homework.

18. a. Mrs. Smith doesn't play golf anymore.
    b. Mrs. Smith never played golf.
    c. Mrs. Smith is going to learn to play golf.

19. a. Jane wanted the dress.
    b. Mary wanted the dress.
    c. Jane forgot the dress.

20. a. No, it isn't true. It is cheap.
    b. Yes, it is. It's very cheap.
    c. Yes, she does. The state university is the most expensive.

21. a. Peter knows my cousin.
    b. Peter wrote to my cousin.
    c. The teacher wrote to my cousin.

22. a. Dr. Smith left at exactly five o'clock.
    b. Dr. Smith left after seven o'clock.
    c. Dr. Smith left before five o'clock.

23. a. The class is always late.
    b. I am always late to class.
    c. The fat boy is always late.

24. a. Sapphires and rubies are more expensive than diamonds.
    b. Rubies are more expensive than sapphires and diamonds.
    c. Diamonds are more expensive than sapphires and rubies.

25. a. The secretary went to the office before Dr. Brown.
    b. Dr. Brown went to the office before his secretary.
    c. The secretary went to the office after Dr. Brown.

LESSON 8—C

Multiple Choice: *Listen carefully. Choose one answer. Draw a circle around the letter. There will be ten seconds between the sentences. Ready? Begin.*

1. a. The teacher went skiing with Jim and Bill.
    b. Jim and Bill didn't go skiing because the teacher warned them.
    c. Jim and Bob went skiing.

2. a. Mrs. Brown needs more groceries.
    b. Mrs. Brown is not going to go to the store.
    c. Mrs. Brown is going to go to the store.

3. a. John needs to buy a book.
    b. John is going to go to the bookstore although he doesn't need a book.
    c. John is going to the bookstore to buy a book.

4. a. John is not going to go to Detroit.
    b. John may go to Detroit.
    c. John went to Detroit by bus.

5. a. John will probably finish his homework during class.
    b. John probably has finished his homework already.
    c. John won't go to class.

6. a. Mr. Brown didn't go to work because it was too cold.
    b. Mr. Brown went to work in spite of the heat.
    c. Mr. Brown drove to work because it was very cold.

7. a. Mr. Brown can't get his secretary to type this.
    b. I believe Mr. Brown will have his secretary type this.
    c. Mr. Brown doesn't have a secretary.

8. a. Yes, they did.
    b. Yes, they should.
    c. Yes, they should have.

9. a. I know Frank was playing golf.
    b. I think Frank was working.
    c. Frank played golf with me.

10. a. John got some toothpaste last night.
    b. I got some toothpaste for John last night.
    c. We need toothpaste.

11. a. He fixed her car.
    b. He told her where to take the car.
    c. She told him where to take the car.

12. a. The teacher speaks Italian very well.
    b. Bob doesn't speak Italian very well.
    c. Bob speaks Italian very well.

13. a. Peter works very hard.
    b. Peter's mother and father work very hard.
    c. Peter's work is very hard.

14. a. Susan will go to the opera in spite of her homework.
    b. Susan will go to the opera if she doesn't have to study.
    c. Susan didn't have to study so she went to the opera.

15. a. The students never stay at school for lunch.
    b. The students always stay at school for lunch.
    c. If it rains, the students stay at school for lunch.

16. a. Mary went to class by taxi.
    b. Mary may go to class.
    c. Mary called a taxi.

17. a. Peter didn't want me to know.
    b. Peter wanted me to know.
    c. I didn't want to know.

18. a. Susan invited Jane.
    b. Jane invited Susan.
    c. Jane didn't invite Susan.

19. a. The children didn't play outside because of the terrible weather.
    b. The children played outside.
    c. The weather was beautiful.

20. a. Mr. Brown finished the work before the boss came.
    b. Mr. Brown didn't finish the work before the boss came.
    c. The boss will finish the work.

21. a. No, I didn't do my homework.
    b. Yes, I should.
    c. Yes, I should have.

22. a. Mary looked for her shoe last night.
    b. Mary found her shoe last night.
    c. Mary didn't look for her shoe last night.

23. a. I used to play the guitar.
    b. I never have played the guitar.
    c. I would like to learn to play the guitar.

24. a. Mrs. Brown couldn't learn Persian.
    b. Mrs. Brown wants to learn to speak Persian.
    c. Mrs. Brown doesn't want to learn to speak Persian.

25. a. Mary's father speaks careful Spanish.
    b. Mary can't speak Spanish.
    c. Mary speaks careful Spanish.

LESSON 8—D

Multiple Choice: *Listen carefully. Choose one answer. Draw a circle around the letter. There will be ten seconds between the sentences. Ready? Begin.*

1. a. It is fascinating to look at his paintings.
   b. It is fascinating to paint pictures.
   c. Painted pictures are fascinating.

2. a. The famous men spoke rapidly.
   b. The president was visiting.
   c. The president spoke rapidly.

3. a. The swimmer is winning the race.
   b. The swimmer did not win the race.
   c. The swimmer won his first race.

4. a. It is easy to learn to read and to write Latin after you can speak it.
   b. It is easier to read Latin than to write it.
   c. It is easy to learn to read and to write Latin.

5. a. Lunch will be served at 12:15 p.m.
   b. There is going to be a movie after lunch.
   c. The movie will begin at 1:00 p.m.

6. a. Betty seldom comes to class because she stays home to study.
   b. Betty is a poor student because she never does her work.
   c. Betty is not very smart.

7. a. Mr. Brown forgot the actor's name.
   b. Mr. Brown forgot the name of the movie.
   c. Mr. Brown forgot to tell the actor his name.

8. a. The FBI agent was flying in his own plane.
   b. The FBI agent had someone stop the plane.
   c. The FBI agent made the plane stop.

9. a. The boy's name is Johnny Wilson.
   b. Johnny Wilson has a son.
   c. Johnny called Mr. and Mrs. Wilson.

10. a. Sam kept the drums his father gave him.
    b. Sam got the drums this evening.
    c. Sam played the drums all evening.

11. a. The neighbors want to paint their house.
    b. The boy doesn't want his house painted.
    c. The boy started painting the house.

12. a. No, she does.
    b. Yes, she does.
    c. Yes, she hasn't.

13. a. I think the teachers are busy.
    b. I know the teachers aren't busy.
    c. I don't know whether or not the teachers are busy.

14. a. Skating is never any fun.
    b. A person should not skate by himself.
    c. Skating is not the only good idea.

15. a. The teacher was tired all day.
    b. The teacher was tired because she worked at school all day.
    c. The teacher worked at school because she was tired.

16. a. Bill drives for Sam.
    b. Bill likes Sam.
    c. Bill drives fast.

17. a. Mary practices the guitar every day but she has a bad teacher.
    b. Mary practices the guitar every day although she is a good player.
    c. Mary practices the guitar every day because she wants to play better.

18. a. John is going to go to Paris before he flies to New York.
    b. John is going to go to New York before he goes to Paris.
    c. John is going to go to Rome after he goes to Paris.

19. a. John is going to play golf after class.
    b. The boy is going to play golf after class.
    c. The boy goes to class with John.

20. a. The French student has a black beard.
    b. The French student wants someone to paint his car.
    c. The French student has a red car.

21. a. The people chose the prime minister.
    b. The prime minister is very young.
    c. The dishonest people elected the young prime minister.

22. a. Mary did her typing before she went to the play.
    b. Mary did her typing after she went to the play.
    c. Mary didn't do her typing.

23. a. The student wanted to carry the tape recorder.
    b. The student wanted me to carry the tape recorder.
    c. The teacher carried the tape recorder all the way to the library.

24. a. Mary cut herself.
    b. Mary saw herself.
    c. Jim got cut.

25. a. No, I have.
    b. Yes, I haven't.
    c. No, I haven't.

ANSWER KEY

To the Teacher

AN EXAMPLE OF THE FORMAT FOR
READING PART 1 OF A LESSON

Teacher: "Lesson 1–A
Part 1: Listen, Repeat, and Write.
Listen carefully. Repeat the sentence aloud. Listen again. Write the sentence. Listen again. Check your answer. Ready? Begin.
Number One. Repeat. *Is it a knife?*"

(Three second pause while students repeat.)

Teacher: "Write. *Is it a knife?*"

(Ten to fifteen second pause while students write.)

Teacher: "Check. *Is it a knife?*"

(Five second pause while students check what they have written.)

Teacher: "Number Two. Repeat. *Are they from Mexico?*"

(Three second pause while students repeat.)

Teacher: "Write. *Are they from Mexico?*"

(Ten to fifteen second pause while students write.)

Teacher: "Check. *Are they from Mexico?*"

(Five second pause while students check what they have written.)

Continue in this way until all sentences for part 1 have been read. See page 83, part 1, of the answer key for the remaining sentences to be read for lesson 1–A, part 1.

AN EXAMPLE OF THE FORMAT FOR
READING PART 2 OF A LESSON

Teacher: "Part 2: Multiple Choice.
Each sentence will be read only once. A sentence will not be repeated. Listen carefully. Draw a circle around the letter of the correct answer. There is only *one* best answer to each question. Ready? Begin.
Number One. *The students are from Mexico.*"

(Twelve second pause while students circle an answer.)

Teacher: "Number Two. *The teacher has a book.*"

      (Twelve second pause while students circle an answer.)

Teacher: "Number Three. *Do they want a sandwich?*"

      (Twelve second pause while students circle an answer.)

Teacher: "Number Four. *They never drink coffee.*"

Continue in this way until all sentences for part 2 have been read. See page 83, parts 2 and 1, for the remaining sentences to be read for lesson 1–A, part 2.

Notice that either *a, b,* or *c* has been circled in part 2 to indicate the correct answer. Notice that the number in parentheses *following* the correct answer is the number of the sentence which matches it and is found in part 1 above (in the same lesson) *following* the matching number.

For example the sentence for number 1 of part 2—*The students are from Mexico.*—is determined by noting that the number *4* is found in parentheses following the circled answer—*They are from Mexico.* Matching the number four to number four in part 1, the sentence—*The students are from Mexico.*—is found.

To the Student

THE IMPORTANCE OF SELF-CORRECTION

When you finish a lesson, check your answers in this answer key. It is *very* important for you to check your answers. Circle your mistakes. Analyze your errors and discuss them with your teacher. If you have many errors on a lesson, do it a second time. Particular attention should be given to—

suffix errors or omissions (-ed, -es, -s, -'s, -ing, -ly, -er, -est),

function word errors or omissions (articles, prepositions, conjunctions, pronouns, auxiliaries),

spelling, punctuation, capitalization errors.

LESSON 1—A

Part 1—Listen, Repeat, and Write:

1. Is it a knife?
2. Are they from Mexico?
3. Are they students?
4. The students are from Mexico.
5. Is the class small?
6. The teacher has a book.
7. Do you see the picture?
8. Do they want a sandwich?
9. I usually drink milk.
10. They never drink coffee.
11. Bob goes home from school at noon.
12. She studied her lessons.
13. Is Bill in class this morning?
14. They were thirsty.
15. Did you study at the library last night?

Part 2—Multiple Choice:

1. a. He is from Mexico.
   (b.) They are from Mexico. (No. 4)*
   c. It is from Mexico.

2. a. It has it.
   b. They have it.
   (c.) He has it. (No. 6)

3. (a.) Yes, they do. (No. 8)
   b. Yes, they are.
   c. Yes, he does.

4. (a.) They don't drink coffee. (No. 10)
   b. They always drink coffee.
   c. They seldom drink coffee.

5. (a.) Last night. (No. 12)
   b. Now.
   c. Every day.

6. a. Yes, I am.
   b. Yes, I was.
   (c.) Yes, I did. (No. 15)

---

* The number in parentheses is the number of the sentence as found above in part 1.

7. a. Yes, she is.
   b. Yes, it is. (No. 1)
   c. Yes, he is.

8. a. Yes, they are. (No. 3)
   b. Yes, I am.
   c. Yes, we are.

9. a. Yes, it is.
   b. Yes, he is.
   c. Yes, they are. (No. 2)

10. a. Yes, they are.
    b. Yes, it is. (No. 5)
    c. Yes, she is.

11. a. Yes, I do. (No. 7)
    b. Yes, they do.
    c. Yes, you do.

12. a. I always drink milk.
    b. I never drink milk.
    c. I often drink milk. (No. 9)

13. a. Bob is at home.
    b. It is twelve o'clock.
    c. Bob goes home at twelve o'clock. (No. 11)

14. a. Yes, he did.
    b. Yes, he is. (No. 13)
    c. Yes, he was.

15. a. Every day.
    b. Now.
    c. Last night. (No. 14)

LESSON 1—B

Part 1—Listen, Repeat, and Write:

1. Where did they study?
2. Did they study last night?
3. Bill is studying in the language lab.
4. Is she living in New York?
5. Who is using my typewriter?
6. Does he want a soup spoon?
7. When are you going to the show?
8. When are they going to the play?
9. What is she going to do?
10. His friends weren't at the library.
11. They rarely go dancing.
12. Does the store have any snowboots?
13. Is Maria a student?
14. Are you and Bill from Canada?
15. Are they teachers?

Part 2—Multiple Choice:

1. (a.) Yes, they did. (No. 2)
   b. In the library.
   c. Last night.

2. a. No, she isn't living.
   (b.) No, she isn't. (No. 4)
   c. No, she wasn't.

3. (a.) Yes, he wants a spoon. (No. 6)
   b. Yes, he wants a cup.
   c. Yes, he wants some soup.

4. a. Yes, they did.
   b. Yesterday morning.
   (c.) In the library. (No. 1)

5. (a.) He is studying now. (No. 3)
   b. He studied yesterday.
   c. He studies every day.

6. a. Mary has.
   b. Tomorrow.
   (c.) Mary is. (No. 5)

7. a. Last night.
   b. I am.
   (c.) This evening. (No. 7)

8. a. In the morning.
   ⓑ Wash the dishes. (No. 9)
   c. In the house.

9. a. They never go.
   ⓑ They seldom go. (No. 11)
   c. They often go.

10. ⓐ Yes, she is. (No. 13)
    b. Yes, it is.
    c. Yes, he is.

11. a. Yes, it is.
    b. Yes, he is.
    ⓒ Yes, they are. (No. 15)

12. ⓐ Tomorrow night. (No. 8)
    b. Yesterday evening.
    c. At the theatre.

13. a. They are going to go there.
    ⓑ They didn't go there. (No. 10)
    c. They went there.

14. a. Yes, it has books.
    b. No, it has blue snowboots.
    ⓒ Yes, it has some. (No. 12)

15. a. Yes, they are.
    b. Yes, I am.
    ⓒ Yes, we are. (No. 14)

LESSON 1—C

Part 1—Listen, Repeat, and Write:

1. The letter is from Japan.
2. Are the classes large?
3. The students have a class at nine.
4. Do they see the clock?
5. Does he want a book?
6. They usually eat hamburgers.
7. I never eat fish.
8. Mary eats lunch in the dorm at noon.
9. They waited for the bus.
10. Was Ted late to class?
11. She was hungry.
12. Did he go to the play last night?
13. Where did he eat?
14. Did she telephone this morning?
15. Ted is swimming in the pool.

Part 2—Multiple Choice:

1. a. It has it.
   b. They have it. (No. 3)
   c. He has it.

2. a. Yes, they do.
   b. Yes, they are.
   c. Yes, he does. (No. 5)

3. a. I always eat fish.
   b. I seldom eat fish.
   c. I don't eat fish. (No. 7)

4. a. Last night. (No. 9)
   b. Tomorrow.
   c. Now.

5. a. Now.
   b. Last night. (No. 11)
   c. Every day.

6. a. Yes, he did.
   b. This morning.
   c. In the dorm cafeteria. (No. 13)

7. a. He is from Japan.
   b. They are from Japan.
   c. It is from Japan. (No. 1)

8. a. Yes, I do.
   b. Yes, you do.
   c. Yes, they do. (No. 4)

9. a. Yes, they are. (No. 2)
   b. Yes, it is.
   c. Yes, she is.

10. a. They often eat hamburgers. (No. 6)
    b. They always eat hamburgers.
    c. They never eat hamburgers.

11. a. Mary went to the restaurant.
    b. Mary eats at twelve o'clock. (No. 8)
    c. It is twelve o'clock.

12. a. Yes, he is.
    b. Yes, he was. (No. 10)
    c. Yes, he did.

13. a. Yes, he did. (No. 12)
    b. Yes, I did.
    c. Yes, I am.

14. a. He swims every day.
    b. He swam yesterday.
    c. He is swimming now. (No. 15)

15. a. At home.
    b. Yes, she did. (No. 14)
    c. Last night.

LESSON 1—D

Part 1—Listen, Repeat, and Write:

1. Is she living in Detroit?
2. Who is waiting for me?
3. Does he want a wrist watch?
4. When is he going to the concert?
5. When are Bob and Jim going to Detroit?
6. What is he going to do?
7. Her friends weren't at the dorm.
8. She rarely smokes.
9. Does the bookstore have any gloves?
10. Where is he from?

Part 2—Multiple Choice:

1. (a.) Tomorrow night. (No. 5)
   b. Yesterday morning.
   c. On the bus.

2. a. Yes, it has it.
   (b.) Yes, it has some. (No. 9)
   c. No, it has blue gloves.

3. (a.) No, she isn't. (No. 1)
   b. No, she isn't living.
   c. No, she wasn't.

4. a. She never smokes.
   (b.) She seldom smokes. (No. 8)
   c. She often smokes.

5. a. Jim has.
   (b.) Jim is. (No. 2)
   c. Tomorrow.

6. a. In the yard.
   b. This afternoon.
   (c.) Wash the car. (No. 6)

7. (a.) Yes, he wants a watch. (No. 3)
   b. What time is it?
   c. Yes, she wants a watch.

89

8. a. They went there.
   b. They are going to go there.
   c. They didn't go there. (No. 7)

9. a. I'm from Venezuela.
   b. She's from Venezuela.
   c. He's from Venezuela. (No. 10)

10. a. He is.
    b. Last night.
    c. This evening. (No. 4)

LESSON 2—A

Part 1—Listen, Repeat, and Write:

1. I want a little milk.
2. I don't have much coffee.
3. Food is expensive.
4. None of the students went to the game.
5. She has a few good students.
6. The teacher needs those chairs.
7. Are the students cold?
8. Do you want this coat or the other coat?
9. One teacher is from New York; the others are from Chicago.
10. We need some toothpaste.
11. The teacher says to the students, "Be at the language lab at nine o'clock."
12. The girls took their dog with them.

Part 2—Multiple Choice:

1. a. It is with them. (No. 12)
   b. They are with them.
   c. They are with her.

2. a. Some of them went.
   b. Not any of them went. (No. 4)
   c. Not all of them went.

3. a. The chairs are there. (No. 6)
   b. The chairs are here.
   c. The chair is there.

4. a. The other. (No. 8)
   b. The coats.
   c. The coat.

5. a. Let's buy another.
   b. Let's buy some. (No. 10)
   c. Let's buy them.

6. a. Some teachers are from Chicago. (No. 9)
   b. All the teachers are from Chicago.
   c. One teacher is from Chicago.

7. a. It's nine o'clock now.
   b. The students are at the language lab now.
   c. The students are going to go to the language lab. (No. 11)

8. a. I want a lot of milk.
    (b.) I don't want much milk. (No. 1)
    c. He wants a lot of milk.

9. a. That food is expensive.
    b. Some food is expensive.
    (c.) All food is expensive. (No. 3)

10. a. She is good.
     b. He is good.
     (c.) They are good. (No. 5)

11. a. Yes, she is.
     (b.) Yes, they are. (No. 7)
     c. Yes, it is cold.

12. a. I have a lot of coffee.
     (b.) I have a little coffee. (No. 2)
     c. I don't have coffee.

LESSON 2—B

Part 1—Listen, Repeat, and Write:

1. The teachers asked us some questions.
2. Whom does the teacher explain the words to?
3. The man gave the woman a book.
4. Susan taught the exercise very well.
5. Mary answered the questions correctly.
6. When did the children dress?
7. The book with the red cover is a grammar book.
8. John speaks Spanish rapidly to Maria and George.
9. The cup with the plastic handle is in the box.
10. Which lesson does Mary like?
11. How many teachers went to the lecture?
12. The boy asked the girl a question.

Part 2—Multiple Choice:

1. a. They gave it.
    b. She gave it.
    c. He gave it. (No. 3)

2. a. She corrected the answers.
    b. The questions were correct.
    c. The answers were correct. (No. 5)

3. a. The book is red.
    b. I lost the cover.
    c. The cover is red. (No. 7)

4. a. The cup is plastic.
    b. The handle is plastic. (No. 9)
    c. The box is plastic.

5. a. The teachers.
    b. Very often.
    c. Four teachers. (No. 11)

6. a. We asked the questions.
    b. They asked the questions. (No. 1)
    c. They answered the questions.

7. a. The students. (No. 2)
    b. The words.
    c. The teacher.

8. a. She thinks well.
   (b.) She teaches well.   (No. 4)
   c. She talks well.

9. a. In a hurry.
   b. In the bedroom.
   (c.) In the morning.   (No. 6)

10. (a.) John is a rapid speaker.   (No. 8)
    b. Maria speaks rapidly.
    c. George is a rapid speaker.

11. (a.) He asked it.   (No. 12)
    b. She asked it.
    c. They asked it.

12. a. He does.
    b. The lesson.
    (c.) The vocabulary lesson.   (No. 10)

LESSON 2—C

Part 1—Listen, Repeat, and Write:

1. Did you buy this car or the other car?
2. The teachers give us the directions.
3. He wants a little lunch.
4. Nowadays clothing costs a lot of money.
5. How did the children dress?
6. Are the students ready?
7. One student went to California; the others went to Michigan.
8. How many students went to the hockey game?
9. The father said to his children, "Be at the swimming pool at four o'clock."
10. Which class does Jim have at eight?
11. The book with the plastic cover is on the desk.
12. He doesn't have much milk.

Part 2—Multiple Choice:

1.   a. He wants a lot of lunch.
     b. She wants a lot of lunch.
     (c.) He doesn't want much lunch. (No. 3)

2.   a. In the evening.
     b. In the bedroom.
     (c.) In a hurry. (No. 5)

3. (a.) Some students went to Michigan. (No. 7)
     b. One student went to Michigan.
     c. All the students went to Michigan.

4.   a. The children are at the swimming pool now.
     b. The children are always late.
     (c.) The children are going to the swimming pool. (No. 9)

5.   a. The desk is plastic.
     b. The book is plastic.
     (c.) The cover is plastic. (No. 11)

6.   a. He has a class at eight o'clock.
     (b.) The biology class. (No. 10)
     c. The class.

7.   a. He has a lot of milk.
     (b.) He has a little milk. (No. 12)
     c. He doesn't have any milk.

8. (a.) The other. (No. 1)
   b. The books.
   c. The others.

9. (a.) They gave the directions. (No. 2)
   b. They got the directions.
   c. We gave the directions.

10. a. Some clothing costs a lot of money.
    b. That clothing costs a lot of money.
    (c.) All clothing costs a lot of money. (No. 4)

11. a. Yes, he is.
    b. Yes, she is.
    (c.) Yes, they are. (No. 6)

12. (a.) All the students went to the hockey game. (No. 8)
    b. They seldom go to a hockey game.
    c. The teachers went to the hockey game.

LESSON 2—D

Part 1—Listen, Repeat, and Write:

1. She has a few good dishes.
2. None of the children were hurt.
3. I need these pencils.
4. I need some coffee.
5. The boys have their books with them.
6. Whom did the student explain the exercise to?
7. Mrs. Brown taught the class very well.
8. I answered the question correctly.
9. The box with the green top has a book in it.
10. Susan speaks French rapidly to Henry and Bob.

Part 2—Mulitiple Choice:

1. (a.) The pencils are here.   (No. 3)
   b. The pencils are there.
   c. The pencil is here.

2. (a.) They are with them.   (No. 5)
   b. It is with them.
   c. They are with him.

3. (a.) She teaches well.   (No. 7)
   b. She thinks well.
   c. She talks well.

4. a. The book is green.
   b. The box is green.
   (c.) The top is green.   (No. 9)

5. a. Some of them were hurt.
   b. Not all of them were hurt.
   (c.) Not any of them were hurt.   (No. 2)

6. (a.) Susan is a rapid speaker.   (No. 10)
   b. Henry is a rapid speaker.
   c. Bob is a rapid speaker.

7. a. She is good.
   (b.) They are good.   (No. 1)
   c. It is good.

8. a. Let's buy another.
   (b.) Let's buy some.   (No. 4)
   c. Let's buy them.

9. a.   An exercise.
    b.   The students.   (No. 6)
    c.   Yesterday.

10. a.   I corrected the answer.
     b.   The question was correct.
     c.   The answer was correct.   (No. 8)

Part 1—Listen, Repeat, and Write:

1. May I bring you a cup of coffee?
2. Mary is playing golf and Bob is too.
3. She can't take tennis lessons this summer.
4. John and Mary are swimming but Frank isn't.
5. Tom can't skate and Mary can't either.
6. He called her up.
7. Mr. Brown got his children up.
8. Why did George go to the drugstore?
9. Bob is going to go to Mr. Lane's store in order to buy some beer.
10. Susan surprised her teacher by working hard.
11. How are you going to go to Detroit?
12. How do you wash your dog?
13. Peter and Bob have to read the lesson.
14. Did Mary want to study last night?

Part 2—Multiple Choice:

1. (a.) She's not going to take them. (No. 3)
   b. She is taking them.
   c. She is going to take them.

2. (a.) Mary can't skate. (No. 5)
   b. Tom can skate.
   c. Mary can skate.

3. (a.) He woke them. (No. 7)
   b. He telephoned them.
   c. He waited for them.

4. (a.) He's going for beer. (No. 9)
   b. He's going for Mr. Lane.
   c. He's going for the weekend.

5. a. In the morning.
   b. For fun.
   (c.) By train. (No. 11)

6. (a.) They must read it. (No. 13)
   b. They have it.
   c. They read many of them.

7. (a.) Yes, please bring it to me. (No. 1)
   b. I don't like you.
   c. Yes, I have it.

8. a. Bob played after Mary.
   (b.) Bob is playing golf.   (No. 2)
   c. Bob isn't playing golf.

9. a. Frank is swimming.
   (b.) John is swimming.   (No. 4)
   c. None of them are swimming.

10. a. She visited him
    b. He visited her.
    (c.) He telephoned her.   (No. 6)

11. a. Slowly.
    (b.) For some toothpaste.   (No. 8)
    c. By car.

12. (a.) She worked hard.   (No. 10)
    b. Her teacher worked hard.
    c. They both worked hard.

13. a. No, but she didn't.
    b. No, but she must.
    (c.) No, but she had to.   (No. 14)

14. a. In the evening.
    (b.) With soap and water.   (No. 12)
    c. To look nice.

LESSON 3—B

Part 1—Listen, Repeat, and Write:

1. That coat is too expensive for the girl to buy.
2. The lesson is easy enough for me to learn.
3. He taught her not to speak quickly.
4. John wants his sister to write a letter to him.
5. Who is at the door?
6. There's a plane at twelve o'clock.
7. What is the girl's name?
8. Whose car is this?
9. I have a blue shirt and Bob has a few white ones.
10. Peter's car is as big as John's.
11. The little car is less expensive than the big one.
12. The new car is bad but the old one is worse.
13. My horse is as old as yours.
14. John is a slow swimmer and Mary is just like him.

Part 2—Multiple Choice:

1. a. I can't learn the lesson.
   b. I can learn the lesson. (No. 2)
   c. I don't like the lesson.

2. a. She wants to write a letter.
   b. He wants to write a letter.
   c. He wants a letter from her. (No. 4)

3. a. A plane leaves at twelve o'clock. (No. 6)
   b. A plane leaves at two o'clock.
   c. The plane is over there.

4. a. This is Peter.
   b. It's Peter.
   c. It's mine. (No. 8)

5. a. Peter's is bigger.
   b. John's is bigger.
   c. They are the same size. (No. 10)

6. a. Both are good.
   b. The old one is better.
   c. The new one is better. (No. 12)

7. a. Both swim slowly. (No. 14)
   b. John swims faster than Mary.
   c. Mary swims faster than John.

8. a. She can buy it.
    b. She can't buy it. (No. 1)
    c. She bought it.

9. a. She learned to speak slowly. (No. 3)
    b. He learned to speak slowly.
    c. He taught her slowly.

10. a. She's Mary.
     b. There's Mary.
     c. It's Mary. (No. 5)

11. a. It's Mary. (No. 7)
     b. It's a girl.
     c. It's her name.

12. a. I have some shirts.
     b. He has some shirts. (No. 9)
     c. He has one shirt.

13. a. The little one costs more.
     b. The big one costs more. (No. 11)
     c. They both cost the same.

14. a. My horse is older.
     b. Our horses are the same age. (No. 13)
     c. Your horse is older.

LESSON 3—C

Part 1—Listen, Repeat, and Write:

1. May I bring you a glass of beer?
2. Mary got her sister up.
3. Jim and Bill have to study the vocabulary lesson.
4. Bob is going to go to Mr. Brown's store tomorrow in order to buy a typewriter.
5. Who's at the door?
6. What is the woman's name?
7. Betty is a slow eater and Bob is just like her.
8. The red book is less expensive than the black one.
9. Bob can't drive and Susan can't either.
10. How are you going to Chicago?
11. There's a bus at six o'clock.
12. The new book is bad but the old one is worse.
13. Bob and Susan are students but Mary isn't.
14. Did Bob want to swim last night?

Part 2—Multiple Choice:

1. a. She visited her.
   ⓑ She woke her. (No. 2)
   c. She telephoned her.

2. a. He's going to visit Mr. Brown.
   ⓑ He's going for a typewriter. (No. 4)
   c. He went last week.

3. a. It's a woman.
   ⓑ It's Mrs. Brown. (No. 6)
   c. It's Mr. Brown.

4. a. The red book costs more.
   ⓑ The black book costs more. (No. 8)
   c. They both cost the same.

5. a. In the morning.
   ⓑ By plane. (No. 10)
   c. For a meeting.

6. a. The old one is better.
   b. Both are good.
   ⓒ The new one is better. (No. 12)

7. ⓐ No, but he had to. (No. 14)
   b. No, but he didn't.
   c. No, but he must.

8. a. Yes, I learned it yesterday.
   b. Yes, please bring it to me. (No. 1) ⓑ
   c. I like John.

9. a. They ate it.
   b. They studied it.
   c. They must study it. (No. 3) ⓒ

10. a. It's the teacher. (No. 5) ⓐ
    b. She's the teacher.
    c. There's the teacher.

11. a. Bob eats faster than Betty.
    b. Betty eats faster than Bob.
    c. Both eat slowly. (No. 7) ⓒ

12. a. Bob can drive.
    b. Susan can't drive. (No. 9) ⓑ
    c. Susan can drive.

13. a. The bus leaves at six o'clock. (No. 11) ⓐ
    b. The bus leaves at eight o'clock.
    c. The bus is over there.

14. a. Bob is a student. (No. 13) ⓐ
    b. Mary is a student.
    c. None of them are students.

LESSON 3—D

Part 1—Listen, Repeat, and Write:

1. Susan wants her father to write a letter to her.
2. Whose book is this?
3. Ted surprised his friends by working hard.
4. They can't go to the show tonight.
5. This car is too expensive for the student to buy.
6. Elaine's dress is as short as Mary's.
7. His car is as old as mine.
8. Mary has a large notebook and Jim has a few small ones.
9. She taught him not to speak loudly.
10. The airplane is easy enough for me to fly.
11. How do you polish you shoes?
12. Why did Mary go to the grocery store?
13. The teacher called John up.
14. Betty is skating and Mary is too.

Part 2—Multiple Choice:

1. a. It's Mary.
   b. This is Mary.
   c. It's mine. (No. 2)

2. a. They are not going to go. (No. 4)
   b. They are going to go.
   c. They are late.

3. a. They are the same length. (No. 6)
   b. Mary's dress is longer.
   c. Elaine's dress is longer.

4. a. Jim has one notebook.
   b. Jim has some notebooks. (No. 8)
   c. Mary has some notebooks.

5. a. I like the airplane.
   b. I can fly the airplane. (No. 10)
   c. I can't fly the airplane.

6. a. In a minute.
   b. For a loaf of bread. (No. 12)
   c. Yesterday.

7. a. Mary isn't skating.
   b. Betty isn't skating.
   c. Both are skating. (No. 14)

8. a. He wants to write a letter.
   b. She wants to write a letter.
   ⓒ She wants a letter from him.   (No. 1)

9. a. They worked hard.
   ⓑ He worked hard.   (No. 3)
   c. She worked hard.

10. ⓐ He can't buy it.   (No. 5)
    b. He can buy it.
    c. He bought it.

11. a. My car is newer.
    b. His car is older.
    ⓒ The cars are the same age.   (No. 7)

12. a. She learned to speak softly.
    ⓑ He learned to speak softly.   (No. 9)
    c. She taught him to speak loudly.

13. ⓐ With liquid polish.   (No. 11)
    b. In the morning.
    c. In the kitchen.

14. ⓐ The teacher telephoned John.   (No. 13)
    b. The teacher visited John.
    c. John telephoned the teacher.

LESSON 4—A

Part 1—Listen, Repeat, and Write:

1. The man who saved Mary was rewarded.
2. What did John and Bob do while Margaret was shopping?
3. I called Bob while John was playing tennis.
4. Maria is the student that Mrs. Smith visited.
5. Mary and Margaret came after I went home.
6. Do you remember who saw Mary?
7. Do you know who visited Bill?
8. Do you think that they are going to go to Detroit Wednesday evening?
9. Mr. Johnson doesn't know I'm here.
10. I remember the name of the record you bought.
11. I have studied chemistry for three years now.
12. Bob has been living in Chicago for ten years.

Part 2—Multiple Choice:

1. a. She was swimming.
   b. He was working
   c. They were playing tennis. (No. 2)

2. a. Maria visited Mrs. Smith.
   b. Mrs. Smith visited Maria. (No. 4)
   c. Maria visited the teacher.

3. a. Yes, I remember Mary.
   b. Mr. Brown saw her. (No. 6)
   c. She saw Mr. Brown.

4. a. Yes, I think she'll go.
   b. Yes, I think it is.
   c. Yes, I think they'll go. (No. 8)

5. a. I bought the record.
   b. I remember you.
   c. I remember the title of the record. (No. 10)

6. a. He left there ten years ago.
   b. He is going to live there for ten years.
   c. He is living there now. (No. 12)

7. a. The man was rewarded. (No. 1)
   b. Mary was rewarded.
   c. The men were rewarded.

8. (a.) I called Bob. (No. 3)
   b. I called John.
   c. Bob called John.

9. (a.) I didn't see them. (No. 5)
   b. I saw them.
   c. They saw me.

10. (a.) Peter visited him. (No. 7)
    b. He visited Peter.
    c. George is a dentist.

11. a. I'm going home.
    b. Mr. Johnson isn't here.
    (c.) I'm here. (No. 9)

12. (a.) I began three years ago. (No. 11)
    b. I finished three years ago.
    c. I am starting now.

LESSON 4—B

Part 1—Listen, Repeat, and Write:

1. I have been studying grammar for two hours.
2. Peter hadn't gone to the language lab before he went swimming.
3. Have the women used the telephone this afternoon?
4. Had you called Mary before she called you?
5. Peter is going to be left at his friend's house.
6. Bob isn't here any more.
7. Professor Brown is a fascinating teacher.
8. Bob's teacher said he is a surprising student.
9. Bob heard an interesting speaker last night.
10. Mary is used to studying grammar.
11. The girl who kicked John was crying.
12. What did Frank and Peter do while Mary stayed home?
13. I visited Mary while John was at work.

Part 2—Multiple Choice:

1. a. He went to the language lab.
   (b.) He went swimming. (No. 2)
   c. He went to the language lab and he went swimming.

2. a. Yes, I would have.
   b. Yes, I have.
   (c.) Yes, I had. (No. 4)

3. (a.) He has left already. (No. 6)
   b. He's still here.
   c. He isn't here yet.

4. (a.) Bob's teacher is surprised. (No. 8)
   b. The student is surprised.
   c. Bob is surprised.

5. a. Mary has stopped studying grammar.
   b. Mary is going to begin studying grammar.
   (c.) Mary studies grammar. (No. 10)

6. a. She was at work.
   b. He was working.
   (c.) They were skiing. (No. 12)

7. a. I am going to study for two hours.
   b. I stopped studying for two hours.
   (c.) I am studying now. (No. 1)

8. a. No, they aren't.
   b. No, they hadn't.
   c. No, they haven't. (No. 3)

9. a. Peter will visit his friend. (No. 5)
   b. He will leave his friend.
   c. His friend will leave.

10. a. He is fascinated.
    b. His students are fascinating.
    c. His students are fascinated. (No. 7)

11. a. I was interesting.
    b. He was interested. (No. 9)
    c. I was interested.

12. a. The girl was crying. (No. 11)
    b. John was crying.
    c. The girls were crying.

13. a. I visited Mary. (No. 13)
    b. I visited John.
    c. John visited Mary.

LESSON 4—C

Part 1—Listen, Repeat, and Write:

1. Mrs. Walker is the teacher that Bob telephoned.
2. The new students left before I came.
3. Do you remember who telephoned Bob?
4. Do you know who called Peter?
5. Do you think that they are going to go to the show tonight?
6. Mr. Borman doesn't know she's here.
7. I remember the name of the movie you saw.
8. I have studied English for one year now.
9. Mary has been living in Detroit for five years.
10. Betty has been watching TV for half an hour.
11. Bob hadn't gone to the store before he went skiing.
12. Have the men used the dynamite today?

Part 2—Multiple Choice:

1. (a.) I didn't meet them.   (No. 2)
   b. I met them.
   c. They met me.

2. (a.) Mary called him.   (No. 4)
   b. He called Mary.
   c. He called his mother.

3. a. She's not here.
   b. Mr. Borman isn't here.
   (c.) She's here.   (No. 6)

4. (a.) I began one year ago.   (No. 8)
   b. I finished one year ago.
   c. I am beginning now.

5. a. She is going to watch for half an hour.
   b. She stopped watching for half an hour.
   (c.) She is watching now.   (No. 10)

6. a. No, they aren't.
   b. No, they hadn't.
   (c.) No, they haven't.   (No. 12)

7. (a.) Bob telephoned the teacher.   (No. 1)
   b. The teacher telephoned Bob.
   c. Mrs. Walker telephoned Bob.

8. a. Yes, I remember Bob.
   ⓑ Mr. Johnson telephoned him.   (No. 3)
   c. He telephoned Mr. Johnson.

9. a. Yes, I think I'll go.
   b. Yes, I think she will go.
   ⓒ Yes, I think they'll go.   (No. 5)

10. a. I saw the movie.
    b. I remember you.
    ⓒ I remember the title of the movie.   (No. 7)

11. a. She left there five years ago.
    b. She is going to live there for five years.
    ⓒ She is living there now.   (No. 9)

12. a. He went to the store.
    ⓑ He went skiing.   (No. 11)
    c. He went to the store and he went skiing.

LESSON 4—D

Part 1—Listen, Repeat, and Write:

1. Had you spoken to Bob before he spoke to you?
2. John is going to be left at his brother's house.
3. Mr. and Mrs. Williams aren't here any more.
4. Professor Smith is a boring teacher.
5. Betty's teacher said she is a surprising student.
6. I saw a frightening animal last night.
7. Bob is used to smoking cigars.
8. What did Betty do while Peter and Jim were skating?
9. Helen is the girl that Bob visited.
10. I heard an inspiring speaker last night.
11. Mr. Miller doesn't teach here any more.
12. Bob is used to drinking coffee.
13. The boy who hit the teacher was laughing.

Part 1—Multiple Choice:

1. a. John will visit his brother. (No. 2)
   b. He will leave his brother.
   c. His brother will leave John.

2. a. He's bored.
   b. His students are boring.
   c. His students are bored. (No. 4)

3. a. I was frightened. (No. 6)
   b. The animal was frightened.
   c. I was frightening.

4. a. She was writing letters. (No. 8)
   b. They were writing letters.
   c. He was skating.

5. a. I was inspiring.
   b. I was inspired. (No. 10)
   c. The speaker was tired.

6. a. Bob has stopped drinking coffee.
   b. Bob is going to begin drinking coffee.
   c. Bob drinks coffee. (No. 12)

7. a. Yes, I would have.
   b. Yes, I have.
   c. Yes, I had. (No. 1)

8. (a.) They have left already. (No. 3)
   b. They're still here.
   c. They aren't here yet.

9. (a.) Betty's teacher is surprised. (No. 5)
   b. Betty is surprised.
   c. Everybody went to lunch.

10. a. Bob has stopped smoking cigars.
    b. Bob is going to begin smoking cigars.
    (c.) Bob smokes cigars. (No. 7)

11. (a.) Bob visited the girl. (No. 9)
    b. The girl visited Bob.
    c. Helen visited Bob.

12. (a.) He has left already. (No. 11)
    b. He's still here.
    c. He isn't here yet.

13. (a.) The boy was laughing. (No. 13)
    b. The teacher was laughing.
    c. The boys were laughing.

LESSON 5—A

Part 1—Listen, Repeat, and Write:

1. He lets his students listen to the news broadcast.
2. You must make students study grammar.
3. My father wishes he could fly an airplane.
4. I asked him how to fix my car.
5. Mary promised to tell me where to find the shoestore.
6. I wish I spoke Spanish.
7. Mrs. Smith should have picked up her husband.
8. Might you have been reading when I telephoned?
9. Should we have brought our books to class?
10. Jim wished he had brought his notebook to class.
11. I didn't hear you knock. I must have been thinking about my girl friend.
12. I go to bed at twelve o'clock unless I watch the television movie.
13. Mary continued to talk although the class had begun.
14. I watch TV whether or not the show is good.

Part 2—Multiple Choice:

1. a. He can fly.
   b. He could fly.
   c. He can't fly. (No. 3)

2. a. Mary told me where it is.
   b. I know where it is.
   c. Mary knows where it is. (No. 5)

3. a. She will get her husband.
   b. She got her husband.
   c. She didn't get her husband. (No. 7)

4. a. Yes, we should.
   b. Yes, we should have. (No. 9)
   c. Yes, we did.

5. a. I wasn't thinking.
   b. I was thinking. (No. 11)
   c. I have to think.

6. a. She talked until it began.
   b. She talked after it began. (No. 13)
   c. She talked because it began.

7. a. They must listen.
   b. They may listen. (No. 1)
   c. They don't listen.

115

8. a. You must study grammar.
   b. John must study.
   ⓒ They must study grammar. (No. 2)

9. a. I asked him to fix my car.
   b. He wants to fix my car.
   ⓒ I want to fix my car. (No. 4)

10. a. I can speak Spanish.
    ⓑ I cannot speak Spanish. (No. 6)
    c. I spoke Spanish.

11. a. Yes, I might.
    ⓑ Yes, I might have. (No. 8)
    c. Yes, I might be.

12. ⓐ He didn't bring it. (No. 10)
    b. He brought it.
    c. He forgot his pencil.

13. a. I always go to bed at twelve o'clock.
    b. I always watch the television movie.
    ⓒ I sometimes go to bed after twelve o'clock. (No. 12)

14. ⓐ I always watch TV. (No. 14)
    b. I watch unless the show is bad.
    c. I watch because the shows are bad.

LESSON 5—B

Part 1—Listen, Repeat, and Write:

1. The students went to class in spite of the cold weather.
2. I'm going to go to Los Angeles although it's far away.
3. Why aren't you going to the movies?
4. Susan will go by plane if she goes to New York next month.
5. If Bob had caught the plane, he would be here by now.
6. Mary would have stayed for dinner last night if we had asked her.
7. I would go to the party if I got a new dress.
8. John is going to go to class whether or not he can finish his homework.
9. Betty would have cashed my check if the bank had been open.
10. I have so little money I can't spend much on clothes.
11. Bob says, "Weren't you able to go by bus?" Betty says, "No."
12. Mr. Smith is so busy that Sam should help him.
13. Mary says, "The grammar book isn't yours, is it?" Betty says, "Yes."
14. Mrs. Smith says, "Can't we begin the class at nine o'clock?" Bob says, "Yes."
15. Mary says, "They sell cigarettes in drugstores, don't they?" Betty says, "Yes."

Part 2—Multiple Choice:

1. a. Los Angeles is near.
   b. I'm going far away. (No. 2)
   c. I'm not going to go to Los Angeles.

2. a. Susan went to New York by plane.
   b. Susan has gone to New York.
   c. Susan might go to New York. (No. 4)

3. a. Mary stayed for dinner.
   b. We didn't ask Mary to stay for dinner. (No. 6)
   c. We asked Mary to stay for dinner.

4. a. He will go. (No. 8)
   b. He may go.
   c. He won't go.

5. a. I spend too much on clothes.
   b. I have too many clothes.
   c. I am too poor to buy many clothes. (No. 10)

6. a. Sam is helping him.
   b. Sam ought to help him. (No. 12)
   c. Sam is busy.

7. a. They can. (No. 14)
   b. They can't.
   c. They should.

117

8. (a.) They went although it was cold. (No. 1)
    b. They went because of the weather.
    c. It was too cold to go.

9. a. In spite of my test tomorrow.
    (b.) Because of my test tomorrow. (No. 3)
    c. Unless I have a test tomorrow.

10. a. He is here now.
     b. He caught the plane.
     (c.) He didn't catch the plane. (No. 5)

11. a. I got a new dress.
     b. I didn't go to the party.
     (c.) I need a new dress. (No. 7)

12. (a.) Betty didn't cash a check. (No. 9)
     b. Betty cashed a check.
     c. I cashed a check.

13. a. Betty could go by bus.
     (b.) Betty couldn't go by bus. (No. 11)
     c. Betty went by bus.

14. a. It is Mary's.
     (b.) It is Betty's. (No. 13)
     c. It isn't Betty's.

15. a. They don't sell them.
     b. They sold them.
     (c.) They sell them. (No. 15)

LESSON 5—C

Part 1—Listen, Repeat, and Write:

1. My father lets me drive the car.
2. We must make children take baths.
3. My sister wishes she could ride a bicycle.
4. I asked her how to cook the meat.
5. Bob agreed to tell me where to find the East Engineering Building.
6. Betty wishes she spoke Italian.
7. Mary should have gotten her cleaning.
8. Might Frank have been sleeping when I telephoned?
9. Should we have studied the reading lesson?
10. Mary wished she had brought her dog to school.
11. I didn't hear the telephone ring. I must have been thinking about my work.
12. I go to bed at ten o'clock unless I am visiting friends.
13. Bob continued to study although the vacation had begun.
14. John eats at the Union whether or not the food is good.

Part 2—Multiple Choice:

1. a. You must take baths.
    b. We must take baths.
    c. They must take baths. (No. 2)

2. a. I asked her to cook the meat.
    b. She wants to cook the meat.
    c. I want to cook the meat. (No. 4)

3. a. She can speak Italian.
    b. She cannot speak Italian. (No. 6)
    c. She spoke Italian.

4. a. Yes, he might.
    b. Yes, he might have. (No. 8)
    c. Yes, he might be.

5. a. She didn't bring it. (No. 10)
    b. She brought it.
    c. She didn't go to school.

6. a. I always go to bed at ten o'clock.
    b. I always visit friends.
    c. I sometimes go to bed after ten o'clock. (No. 12)

7. a. He always eats at the Union. (No. 14)
    b. He eats at the Union unless the food is bad.
    c. He eats at the Union because the food is bad.

8. a. I must drive the car.
    b. I may drive the car. (No. 1)
    c. I don't drive the car.

9. a. She can ride.
    b. She could ride.
    c. She can't ride. (No. 3)

10. a. Bob told me where it is.
     b. I know where it is.
     c. Bob knows where it is. (No. 5)

11. a. She will get her cleaning.
     b. She got her cleaning.
     c. She didn't get her cleaning. (No. 7)

12. a. Yes, we should.
     b. Yes, we should have. (No. 9)
     c. Yes, we studied.

13. a. I wasn't thinking.
     b. I was thinking. (No. 11)
     c. I have to think.

14. a. He studied until it began.
     b. He studied after it began. (No. 13)
     c. He studied because it began.

LESSON 5—D

Part 1—Listen, Repeat, and Write:

1. John went to class in spite of the dangerous student riots.
2. Frank's going to go to Tokyo although it's far away.
3. Why aren't you going to the meeting?
4. Bob will go by train if he goes to Detroit next week.
5. If Mrs. Smith had caught the train, she would be here by now.
6. Frank would have stayed for lunch if we had asked him.
7. Bob would go to the dance if he got a new suit.
8. Helen is going to go to class whether or not she can finish her research paper.
9. Frank would have returned my book if the door had been open.
10. Students have so little money they can't spend much on movies.
11. Frank says, "Weren't you able to go by train?" Betty says, "No."
12. Bob says, "The Latin books aren't yours, are they?" Frank says, "Yes."
13. Mrs. Lane is so busy that Mary should help her.
14. Mrs. Lane says, "Can't we begin the meeting at ten o'clock?" Mary says, "Yes."
15. John says, "They sell notebooks in book stores, don't they?" Sam says, "Yes."

Part 2—Multiple Choice:

1. a. In spite of my test tomorrow.
    b. Because of my examination tomorrow. (No. 3)
    c. Unless I have a test tomorrow.

2. a. She is here now.
    b. She caught the train.
    c. She didn't catch the train. (No. 5)

3. a. He got a new suit.
    b. He didn't go to the dance.
    c. He needs a new suit. (No. 7)

4. a. Frank didn't return my book. (No. 9)
    b. Frank returned my book.
    c. I returned a book.

5. a. Betty could go by train.
    b. Betty went by train.
    c. Betty couldn't go by train. (No. 11)

6. a. Mary is helping her.
    b. Mary ought to help her. (No. 13)
    c. Mary is busy.

7. a. They don't sell them.
    b. They sold them.
    c. They sell them. (No. 15)

8. (a.) He went although it was dangerous. (No. 1)
   b. He went because of the riots.
   c. It was too dangerous to go.

9. a. Tokyo is near.
   (b.) He's going far away. (No. 2)
   c. He's not going to go to Tokyo.

10. a. Bob went to Detroit by train.
    b. Bob has gone to Detroit.
    (c.) Bob might go to Detroit. (No. 4)

11. a. Frank stayed for lunch.
    (b.) We didn't ask Frank to stay for lunch. (No. 6)
    c. We asked Frank to stay for lunch.

12. (a.) She will go. (No. 8)
    b. She may go.
    c. She won't go.

13. a. They spend too much on movies.
    b. They see too many movies.
    (c.) They are too poor to see many movies. (No. 10)

14. a. They are Bob's.
    (b.) They are Frank's. (No. 12)
    c. They aren't Frank's.

15. (a.) They can. (No. 14)
    b. They can't.
    c. They shouldn't.

LESSON 6—A

Part 1—Listen, Repeat, and Write:

1. What are you looking at in the water?
2. Bob likes to help his father, but he avoids washing the car.
3. Sam kept eating until he finished.
4. The secretary typed Betty's paper, but John typed his paper himself.
5. Mary is watching her mother make a hat for herself.
6. The people elected Kennedy their president.
7. My brother found animals frightening.
8. What do you want done to your watch?
9. Bob read a book describing life at a French university.
10. The president appointed Betty secretary.
11. Mr. Lane watched the boys ice skating in the park.

Part 2—Multiple Choice:

1. a. He is eating.
   b. He is finished.   (No. 3)
   c. He kept it.

2. a. Mary's mother is making a hat for Mary.
   b. Mary is making a hat for herself.
   c. Mary's mother is making a hat for herself.   (No. 5)

3. a. He was frightened.   (No. 7)
   b. The animals were frightened.
   c. He found several animals.

4. a. Bob read about a French university.   (No. 9)
   b. Bob is going to a French university.
   c. Bob described life at a French university.

5. a. Mr. Lane was ice skating with the boys.
   b. The boys were watching Mr. Lane.
   c. Mr. Lane was watching the boys ice skating.   (No. 11)

6. a. I'm looking for the water.
   b. I'm looking at the water myself.
   c. I'm looking at myself in the water.   (No. 1)

7. a. Bob likes to wash the car.
   b. Bob's father likes to wash the car.
   c. Bob doesn't wash the car.   (No. 2)

8. a. The secretary typed John's paper.
   b. John typed his own paper.   (No. 4)
   c. Betty typed her own paper.

9. a. Kennedy elected them.
   b. Kennedy selected the people.
   ⓒ The people chose Kennedy. (No. 6)

10. a. I want a clean watch.
    ⓑ I want it cleaned. (No. 8)
    c. I want to clean it.

11. a. The president is the secretary.
    ⓑ Betty is the secretary. (No. 10)
    c. Betty chose the secretary.

LESSON 6—B

Part 1—Listen, Repeat, and Write:

1. Studying all night on Wednesday made Bill tired on Thursday.
2. Having bought a present for John, Mary went home early.
3. Watching TV made Mary forget to do her reading assignment.
4. Mrs. Brown directed the boy trying to find the office.
5. Writing the word on the blackboard, the student explained to the class what it meant.
6. My parents are coming, therefore I can't go swimming this afternoon.
7. Mary is studying now. Later she will call John. Earlier she washed her hair.
8. Bill worked on the car for two hours; he worked at the store for one hour; and he helped his father in the garden for two hours.
9. The Smiths went to New York first; afterwards they spent a week in Washington and another in Miami.
10. Mr. Johnson is a good pilot; however, he flies fast.

Part 2—Multiple Choice:

1. a. Mary bought a present for John. (No. 2)
   b. John went home early.
   c. John bought a present for Mary.

2. a. She was going to the office.
   b. He was going to the office. (No. 4)
   c. She found him.

3. a. My parents are going to visit me. (No. 6)
   b. I am going to go swimming.
   c. My parents are going swimming.

4. a. However, he worked five hours.
   b. In other words, he worked five hours. (No. 8)
   c. So, he worked until five o'clock.

5. a. He's a good pilot but he flies rather fast. (No. 10)
   b. He flies too fast.
   c. He doesn't fly well.

6. a. Bill was tired Wednesday night.
   b. Bill studied Wednesday night. (No. 1)
   c. Bill studied on Thursday.

7. a. She didn't watch TV.
   b. She didn't do her homework. (No.3)
   c. She watched TV after she finished her homework.

8. a. The class explained the word.
   b. The student explained the word. (No. 5)
   c. The student wrote the explanation.

9. (a.) First, she washed her hair.   (No. 7)
    b. First, she studied.
    c. First, she called John.

10. a. They visited New York after Washington.
     b. They visited Washington after Miami.
    (c.) They visited Miami after New York.   (No. 9)

LESSON 6—C

Part 1—Listen, Repeat, and Write:

1. What is the boy looking at in the water?
2. Mary likes to help her mother, but she avoids sweeping the floor.
3. Mr. Smith kept working until he finished.
4. Someone typed Mary's letter, but Bill typed his letter himself.
5. Bob is watching his father build a desk for himself.
6. The students elected John their chairman.
7. My brother found snakes frightening.
8. What do you want done to your car?
9. Mary read a book describing life in a British college.
10. The dictator appointed John treasurer.
11. Mrs. Smith watched the girls swimming in the pool.

Part 2—Multiple Choice:

1. (a.) He is finished. (No. 3)
   b. He is working.
   c. He kept it.

2. a. Bob is building a desk for himself.
   (b.) Bob's father is building a desk for himself. (No. 5)
   c. Bob's father is building a desk for Bob.

3. a. The snakes were frightened.
   b. He found several snakes.
   (c.) He was frightened. (No. 7)

4. a. Mary described life at a British college.
   b. Mary is going to a British college.
   (c.) Mary read about a British college. (No. 9)

5. a. The girls were watching Mrs. Smith.
   (b.) Mrs. Smith was watching the girls swimming. (No. 11)
   c. Mrs. Smith was swimming with the girls.

6. a. He's looking at the water himself.
   (b.) He's looking at himself in the water. (No. 1)
   c. He's looking for the water.

7. (a.) Mary doesn't sweep the floor. (No. 2)
   b. Mary likes to sweep the floor.
   c. Mary's mother likes to sweep the floor.

8. a. Mary typed her own letter.
   b. Someone typed Bill's letter.
   (c.) Bill typed his own letter. (No. 4)

127

9. a. The students chose John.   (No. 6)
    b. John selected the students.
    c. John elected them.

10. a. I want it fixed.   (No. 8)
     b. I want to fix it.
     c. I want a car.

11. a. The dictator is the treasurer.
     b. John chose the treasurer.
     c. John is the treasurer.   (No. 10)

LESSON 6—D

Part 1—Listen, Repeat, and Write:

1. Working all night on Friday made Dick tired on Saturday.
2. Having bought a shirt for Bob, Dick went home early.
3. Playing volleyball made Sam forget to do his grammar assignment.
4. The policeman directed the woman trying to find the library.
5. My brother is coming, therefore I can't play volleyball this evening.
6. Writing the word on the blackboard, the teacher explained to the students what it meant.
7. John is reading now. Later he will call Betty. Earlier he took a bath.
8. Mary worked on homework for two hours; she worked at the library for one hour; and she helped her mother in the kitchen for one hour.
9. The Johnsons went to Los Angeles first; afterwards they spent a week in Tokyo and another in Honolulu.
10. Bill is a good motorcyclist; however, he rides fast.

Part 2—Multiple Choice:

1.   a. Bob went home early.
     (b.) Dick bought a shirt for Bob. (No. 2)
     c. Bob bought a shirt for Dick.

2.   a. He found her.
     b. He found the library.
     (c.) She was going to the library. (No. 4)

3.   a. The teacher wrote the explanation.
     b. The students explained the word.
     (c.) The teacher explained the word. (No. 6)

4.   a. So, she worked until four o'clock.
     b. However, she worked four hours.
     (c.) In other words, she worked four hours. (No. 8)

5. (a.) He's a good rider although he rides rather fast. (No. 10)
     b. He rides too fast.
     c. He isn't a good rider.

6. (a.) Dick worked Friday night. (No. 1)
     b. Dick was tired Friday night.
     c. Dick worked on Saturday.

7.   a. He played volleyball after he finished his homework.
     b. He didn't play volleyball.
     (c.) He didn't do his homework. (No. 3)

8.   a. My brother is playing volleyball.
     (b.) My brother is going to visit me. (No. 5)
     c. I am going to play volleyball.

9. a. First, he called Mary.
   b. First, he took a bath. (No. 7)
   c. First, he read a book.

10. a. They visited Tokyo after Honolulu.
    b. They visited Honolulu after Los Angeles. (No. 9)
    c. They visited Los Angeles after Tokyo.

Multiple Choice:

1. She'd like to see the movie tomorrow. (b)
2. The lesson is easy for Mary to do. (c)
3. The teacher asked us to call on her but we were too busy. (c)
4. It is necessary for children to eat nutritious food. (b)
5. Jim's father was interesting. (b)
6. Mary has two green dresses and two yellow ones. (c)
7. Sam is a fast worker and Jim is just like him. (b)
8. Sally gets good grades in her classes by studying hard. (b)
9. Why did Mary go to Detroit? (c)
10. Susan called up her teacher yesterday afternoon. (c)
11. Bob is going to write to me and Fred is too. (b)
12. Mary mustn't stay here. (c)
13. The teacher expected us not to pass the test. (c)
14. The blue coat is too short for Susan, but it's long enough for Judy. (b)
15. The music teacher gets the students to sing the songs. (b)
16. It's easy for the teachers to speak English. (a)
17. Whose book is this? It's yours, mine is in the closet. (a)
18. The picture on the wall was blue. (b)
19. The boys are the same age, but Peter isn't as tall as John. (a)
20. How did your brother learn Spanish? (b)
21. Fred went to Detroit by bus in order to attend the meeting there yesterday.
    Why did Fred go to Detroit? (a)
22. Frank took the bus to the language lab. He ran into Bob there. (c)
23. Bill can't sing and Susan can't either. (c)
24. Mary doesn't work hard but Jim does. (b)
25. Jim'll go to the meeting at eleven o'clock. (c)

LESSON 7—B

Multiple Choice:

1. I suppose that the teacher wants me to finish the course. (c)
2. Jim had planned to visit his friends but he had to study. (c)
3. Mary has been looking for her cat for half an hour. (c)
4. Betty has begun to study French. (b)
5. John and Peter are needed to finish the job. (a)
6. The students don't go to the lab anymore. (b)
7. The movie frightened Jane. (c)
8. Susan remembers when her father played chess with her mother. (a)
9. Peter and Susan studied for three hours after dinner. (c)
10. John went to the library while Peter was swimming. (b)
11. The concert we attended last night was interesting. (a)
12. Bob left the lab fifteen minutes ago. Betty left sooner than he did. (b)
13. They have been working for six hours. (a)
14. Jane had intended to buy a new dress but she didn't have enough money. (c)
15. Margaret hasn't seen Jim since he came to the university. (c)
16. The story was explained to Mary and Jack yesterday. (c)
17. The students haven't eaten lunch yet. (a)
18. Bill drinks coffee and Peter used to. (c)
19. Bob forgot which tie Sam wanted. (a)
20. Do you know which student is the most intelligent? (c)
21. Mary knows the student who spoke to my brother. (a)
22. Fred stayed at the lab until ten o'clock. (b)
23. The pretty girl who rides the bus each day is always smiling. (a)
24. Jane and Sally are beautiful but Mary is the most beautiful of all. (b)
25. Jane went to class at ten o'clock. John went earlier than she did. (b)

LESSON 7—C

Multiple Choice:

1. Bill will go to the bookstore whether or not he's going to need more books. (a)
2. Bob went to the movies in spite of his father's objections. (b)
3. Bill isn't going to the lab although he needs to study the lessons. (c)
4. Mr. Brown'll go by bus if he goes to work today. (a)
5. Peter would have bought the tickets before he went to the game. (b)
6. It was such a nice day that Mr. Brown walked to work. (b)
7. John can get Mary to play this can't he? (a)
8. Should he fix the car? (a)
9. The girls must have been studying while the boys were swimming. (c)
10. Susan should have bought some bread yesterday. (a)
11. The teacher told us where to get the tickets. (c)
12. John wishes that he were able to speak English better. (b)
13. Professor Wilson makes them study very hard. (b)
14. Peter will go to the lab unless he has to work. (a)
15. Betty drives to work whenever it rains. (c)
16. Jim would go by plane if he went to New York. (c)
17. Mary would have called me if I had wanted her to. (b)
18. Fred would have called Bill if he had wanted him to. (c)
19. It was such a beautiful day that we went on a picnic. (a)
20. Jim wishes he could have finished the work before his father came home. (b)
21. Should the teacher have bought the beer? (c)
22. He could have looked for the book this morning. (a)
23. Mary forgot how to ride a bicycle. (c)
24. The students who don't speak English wish they could learn it. (b)
25. His teacher made him speak correct English. (a)

LESSON 7—D

Multiple Choice:

1. Mary goes to church with that girl playing the piano. (a)
2. Working rapidly, the man wrote a poem for the beautiful girl visiting him. (a)
3. Having sold his first book, Jim was very happy. (c)
4. It is hard to learn to read Russian. It is also hard to learn to speak and write it. (c)
5. Breakfast is going to be at 7:30. Later in the morning there's going to be a meeting. (c)
6. Mary doesn't like to study, and therefore never does her lab work. She seldom does her home-work either. In other words she's just not a very good student. (b)
7. Betty forgot the name of the student standing by the door. (c)
8. The detective had the truck stopped. (c)
9. Peter calls his dog Buster. (b)
10. The students kept on studying the lessons all afternoon. (a)
11. Dad started fixing the car himself. (c)
12. Does the secretary have a lot of typing to do? (b)
13. John and Frank aren't thirsty. (b)
14. Writing songs can be fun. (c)
15. Having worked at the hospital all day, the doctor was tired. (b)
16. I would have stopped him if the policeman had wanted me to. (c)
17. Bob is a poor swimmer now, but he wants to become a good swimmer. Therefore, he practices every day. (b)
18. My parents are going to Montreal. Afterwards they're going to London and then they'll fly to Paris. (a)
19. Skiing alone is never a good idea. (c)
20. We made Mary our secretary although she's very young. (b)
21. When Bob finished working, he went to the lecture. (c)
22. Jim insisted on carrying Mary's books all the way to the lab. (c)
23. Billy watched his father shave himself. (c)
24. Haven't you explained to the teacher yet? (b)
25. The policeman with the broken leg wants his house painted green. (c)

LESSON 8—A

Multiple Choice:

1. He'd like to see the doctor as soon as possible. (a)
2. The job is easy for John to finish. (b)
3. We asked the Andersons to call on us, but they were too busy. (b)
4. It's necessary for them to learn English. (c)
5. Mary's pictures of her trip were interesting. (c)
6. The millionaire has two black cars and two white cars. (b)
7. Mr. Brown is a good driver and his wife is just like him. (c)
8. Mr. Smith gets along well with his boss by working hard. (c)
9. Why did Peter go to Spain? (b)
10. Jim called up his girl friend last night. (b)
11. My mother is going to write to me and my father is too. (a)
12. Betty mustn't leave. (c)
13. My father expected me not to miss the bus. (c)
14. The house was too small for the Smith family but it was big enough for the Anderson family. (c)
15. The coach gets the football team to learn the plays. (c)
16. It's easy for children to learn a new language. (c)
17. Whose notebook is this? It must be yours, mine's at home. (b)
18. The cover on the box I lost was green. (a)
19. Mary and Jane are in the same class, but Mary isn't as old as Jane. (c)
20. How did you learn to play the violin? (c)
21. Dr. Brown went to New York by train in order to attend the meeting there last week. Why did Dr. Brown go to New York? (b)
22. Sam walked to the library. He ran into Bill on the way. (a)
23. I can't play the piano and Mary can't either. (c)
24. John doesn't swim well but Frank does. (a)
25. Bob'll go to the lab at seven o'clock. (c)

LESSON 8—B

Multiple Choice:

1. I suppose that my mother wants me to finish my dinner. (b)
2. We had wanted to drive to Detroit today but we had to work. (c)
3. Jim has been looking for his tennis racket for ten minutes. (b)
4. Bob has begun to study medicine. (b)
5. Mary and Susan are needed to finish the typing. (b)
6. Mr. Smith doesn't go to movies any more. (c)
7. The lecture bored the students. (a)
8. Peter remembers when Bill played golf with his father. (a)
9. Mr. Anderson and his secretary worked for three hours after lunch. (c)
10. Mrs. Brown went to the store while her husband was working. (c)
11. The football game we watched on Saturday was exciting. (b)
12. Mrs. Smith left the house an hour ago. Mr. Smith left sooner than she did. (c)
13. We have been studying for four hours. (b)
14. Mr. Brown had intended to buy a new car but he didn't have enough money. (b)
15. John hasn't seen Maria since she came to the ELI. (b)
16. The exercise was explained to the students yesterday. (c)
17. She hasn't done her homework yet. (b)
18. Mr. Smith plays golf and Mrs. Smith used to. (a)
19. Mary forgot which dress Jane wanted. (a)
20. Does Mrs. Murphy know which college is the most expensive? (c)
21. Peter knows the teacher who wrote to my cousin. (c)
22. Doctor Smith stayed at the hospital until five o'clock. (a)
23. The fat boy who sits beside me in class is always late. (c)
24. Sapphires and rubies are expensive but diamonds are the most expensive of all. (c)
25. Doctor Brown went to his office at nine o'clock. His secretary went earlier than he did. (a)

LESSON 8—C

Multiple Choice:

1. Jim and Bill went skiing in spite of their teacher's warning. (c)
2. Mrs. Brown will go to the grocery store whether or not she is going to need more groceries. (c)
3. Jim is not going to the bookstore although he needs to buy a book. (a)
4. John will go by bus if he goes to Detroit today. (b)
5. Bill would have finished the homework before he went to class. (b)
6. It was such a cold day that Mr. Brown drove to work. (c)
7. Mr. Brown can get his secretary to type this, can't he? (b)
8. Should Mr. and Mrs. Johnson buy the car? (b)
9. Frank must have been working while I was playing golf. (b)
10. John should have got some toothpaste last night. (c)
11. He told her where to take the car. (b)
12. The teacher wishes that Bob were able to speak Italian better. (b)
13. Peter's mother and father make him work very hard. (a)
14. Susan will go to the opera unless she has to study. (b)
15. The students stay at school for lunch whenever it rains. (c)
16. Mary would go by taxi if she went to class. (b)
17. Peter would have told me if he had wanted me to know. (a)
18. Jane would have invited Susan if she had wanted her to. (c)
19. It was such terrible weather that the children played inside. (a)
20. Mr. Brown wishes he could have finished the work before the boss came. (b)
21. Should I have done my homework last night? (c)
22. Mary could have looked for her shoe last night. (c)
23. I forgot how to play the guitar. (a)
24. Mrs. Brown, who doesn't speak Persian, wishes she could learn it. (b)
25. Mary's father made her speak careful Spanish. (c)

LESSON 8—D

Multiple Choice:

1. Painting pictures can be fascinating. (b)
2. Speaking rapidly, the president made a speech for the famous men visiting him. (c)
3. Having won his first race, the swimmer was very happy. (c)
4. It is easy to learn to read Latin. It is also easy to learn to write it. (c)
5. Lunch is going to be at 1:00 p.m. Later in the afternoon there's going to be a movie. (b)
6. Betty doesn't like to study English and therefore never does her grammar. She seldom does her reading either. In other words she just isn't a very good student. (b)
7. Mr. Brown forgot the name of the actor appearing in the movie. (a)
8. The FBI agent had the plane stopped. (b)
9. Mr. and Mrs. Wilson call their baby Johnny. (a)
10. Sam kept on playing the drums all night. (c)
11. The boy started painting the house himself. (c)
12. Does Mary have a lot of studying to do? (b)
13. The grammar teachers aren't busy. (b)
14. Skating alone is never a good idea. (b)
15. Having worked at school all day, the teacher was tired. (b)
16. Sam is a fast driver and Bill is just like him. (c)
17. Mary is a poor guitar player now but she wants to become a good player. Therefore she practices every day. (c)
18. John is going to Rome. Afterwards he's going to Paris and then he'll fly to New York. (a)
19. John goes to class with that boy playing golf. (c)
20. The French student with the red beard wants his car painted blue. (b)
21. The people made him their prime minister although he's very dishonest. (a)
22. When Mary finished typing she went to the play. (a)
23. The student insisted on carrying the tape recorder all the way to the library. (a)
24. Mary saw Jim cut himself. (c)
25. Haven't you spoke to Jim yet? (c)